# Praise for
## *Understanding Love and Responsibility*

"Spinello has provided us a marvelously compelling and timely guide to Saint John Paul II's masterpiece *Love and Responsibility*. What a treat to read! The Theology of the Body Institute has long extolled the rich beauty of John Paul II's foundational masterpiece on human love and sexuality. We share Spinello's passion for making this known far and wide to a culture unmoored from a coherent sexual ethic or even a language for love. A great debt is owed to Spinello for his balance of scholarship and readability. *Understanding Love and Responsibility* should play a major role in drawing thirsty souls into the mind, heart, and thought of one of civilization's greatest men on the issues of our age. Kudos!"

— Damon Owens, Executive Director, Theology of the Body Institute

"As the resources helping us grasp the theology of the body have multiplied, a lacuna has remained: how can readers understand the essential pre-papal writings of Karol Wojtyła, such as *Love and Responsibility*, other than by getting an advanced degree in philosophy? Richard Spinello's Companion does a huge service by providing a solid, philosophically informed reading of Wojtyła's crucial text. If you really want to understand the theology of the body, you need to understand *Love and Responsibility*. Now you can, even without a philosophy degree!"

— Angela Franks, PhD, author of *Contraception and Catholicism: What the Church Teaches and Why*

"Karol Wojtyła's book *Love and Responsibility* is an oasis in a world that is suffering a drought of clear thinking in the realm of sexual ethics. However, his profound insights are often inaccessible to readers because of his complex writing style and the depth of his thought. Thankfully, Richard Spinello has offered the Church a helpful companion to

Wojtyła's classic work. His commentary will help anyone who is looking to absorb the richness of the late Holy Father's thought."

"Particularly valuable are Spinello's reflections on the values of chastity, as the "transparency of interiority," and of spousal love as a lifelong vocation, lived out either in marriage or in the complementary vocation of virginity."

"If John Paul II had a 'theology of the body,' he also had a prior 'philosophy of the body': *Love and Responsibility*. John Paul II was a theologian with a philosopher's heart, and *Love and Responsibility* puts forth what the very core of the nature of human love is.

"Dr. Spinello's companion to *Love and Responsibility* is a winner. With so much interest in the theology of the body, it's only natural that people want to dive into its forerunner as well. Spinello lucidly commentates (with important context and background) on what makes human love so unique, namely, the intrinsic dignity of the human person. Romantic and sexual love between two beings of infinite value has got to be something special!

"Spinello 'undensifies' the often dense work of Papa Wojtyła, enlarging on it and making it even more useful to all."

# UNDERSTANDING
# Love and Responsibility

# UNDERSTANDING
# Love and Responsibility

## A Companion to
## Karol Wojtyła's Classic Work

### RICHARD A. SPINELLO

Pauline
BOOKS & MEDIA
Boston

Library of Congress Cataloging-in-Publication Data

Spinello, Richard A.

Understanding Love and responsibility : a companion to Karol Wojtyla's classic work / by Richard A. Spinello.

pages cm

ISBN 978-0-8198-7805-2 -- ISBN 0-8198-7805-7

1. John Paul II, Pope, 1920-2005. Milosc i odpowiedzialnosc. 2. Sex--Religious aspects--Catholic Church. 3. Love--Religious aspects--Catholic Church. 4. Sexual ethics. 5. Catholic Church--Doctrines. I. Title.

BX1795.S48S65 2014

241'.66--dc23

2014006784

The Scripture quotations contained herein are from the *New Revised Standard Version Bible: Catholic Edition,* copyright © 1989, 1993, Division of Christian Education of the National Council of the Churches of Christ in the United States of America. Used by permission. All rights reserved.

Cover design by Rosana Usselmann

"P" and PAULINE are registered trademarks of the Daughters of St. Paul.

Published by Pauline Books & Media, 50 Saint Pauls Avenue, Boston, MA 02130–3491.

Printed in the U.S.A.

www.pauline.org

Pauline Books & Media is the publishing house of the Daughters of St. Paul, an international congregation of women religious serving the Church with the communications media.

1 2 3 4 5 6 7 8 9                                18 17 16 15 14

For Susan
*Vous et nul autre*

# Contents

# Preface

Long before he was installed as Pope John Paul II, Bishop Karol Wojtyła composed a carefully reasoned reflection on sexual ethics that was aptly titled *Love and Responsibility*. This brilliant account of sexual mores and norms is far more relevant today than when it was composed in the more tranquil cultural milieu of the late 1950s. Anyone who picks up this book will be impressed by its directness, originality, and profound insights into entangled ethical issues. In contrast to his other famous work on the morality of sexual relations known as *Man and Woman He Created Them: A Theology of the Body*, this book is more concise and compressed. Wojtyła presents a sustained, penetrating philosophical argument that pivots on the dichotomy between love and use in sexual relationships. He shows how easy it is for those relationships to become depersonalized when the purpose and meaning of human sexuality become obscured. Ethereal notions of love that occupy the moral landscape are sensibly discounted. Wojtyła also carefully presents a personalist argument against the contraceptive mentality that has shadowed so much of contemporary married life. Yet he never wavers from exalting the power of sensuality and the beauty of marital intimacy. In its convincing conclusion, this book demonstrates why marriage is a moral reality, so that attempts to redefine it are contrary to reason and the natural order

*Love and Responsibility* has been understandably eclipsed by the Pope's engaging work on the theology of the body. While there is considerable overlap between these two books, *Love and Responsibility* has a nuance all its own, and it deserves a much wider audience than it has yet received. John Paul II's reflections on the theology of the body were delivered as 129 catecheses at his Wednesday papal audiences from September 1979 through November 1984. These talks deal with human love in the divine plan and are inspired by Sacred Scripture, especially the first few chapters of Genesis.[1] *Love and Responsibility*, on the other hand, is a work of philosophy, inspired to some extent by the moral philosophy of Immanuel Kant, which helped to open Wojtyła's eyes to the value of personalism. The book's density and occasional complexity, which make it rather opaque at times, probably account for its being neglected. Quite simply, *Love and Responsibility* is not an easy book to read, and rarely does its author give concrete examples to illustrate his arguments. Even Wojtyła's fellow academicians have struggled. Halina Bortnowska, one of the Pope's former students, describes *Love and Responsibility* as his most readable book, yet one that is difficult and challenging.[2] Despite its demanding prose, the book is not an academic exercise in abstraction. When properly understood, its universal vision of sexual morality enlightens us through its wisdom and moral prescription.

This serious problem of inaccessibility has been compounded because there is a dearth of secondary sources available to serve as thorough and reliable commentaries. With some notable exceptions, few scholars and teachers have given the book the concentrated attention it deserves. I hope that *Understanding Love and Responsibility* will fill this conspicuous vacuum. I have written it as a companion piece for anyone setting out to understand the main ideas of *Love and Responsibility*. Such a modest effort can serve as a dependable guide

---

1. For more background see Michael Waldstein's "Introduction" to John Paul II, *Man and Woman He Created Them: A Theology of the Body* (Boston: Pauline Books & Media, 2006), 1–128.

2. Jonathan Kwitny, *Man of the Century* (New York: Henry Holt, 1997), 166.

for readers attempting to navigate the deep riches and occasional rigors of Wojtyła's book.

Another help to readers is a new English translation of *Love and Responsibility* that makes Wojtyła's work more readable and accessible. This new translation by Grzegorz Ignatik offers welcome precision and clarity, and it is used throughout this commentary. Each chapter of *Understanding Love and Responsibility* is collated as closely as possible with the text of the Ignatik translation.[3]

I do not intend *Understanding Love and Responsibility* to be an intricately detailed or exhaustive study, nor an in-depth scholarly analysis. Rather, it sketches out the bold lines of Wojtyła's thought and clears away some of the conceptual difficulties for the serious reader. For the most part, I do not adopt a critical attitude, since I am simply trying to shed light on the coherence of Wojtyła's extended argument. In the closing pages, however, I offer a brief defense of that argument and point out some of its particular strengths.

Those who do take up the challenge of carefully reading *Love and Responsibility* will be amply rewarded. Its pertinence and intellectual vitality are indisputable. Wojtyła's ambitious project succeeds in evoking the question of sexual morality in the most radical terms. The appeal of his approach lies in its reliance on the incomparable value of the human person as the unyielding criterion for evaluating sexual mores and attitudes, and for resolving the peculiar paradoxes of erotic love. The study of *Love and Responsibility* is also indispensable for fully appreciating the legacy of Saint John Paul II, one of the most charismatic and influential popes of the twentieth century. Several of the central themes articulated in this work reappear in his papal encyclicals and other later writings.[4] John Paul II's teachings were a rare voice in the world when he was Pope, but they will continue speaking through books like *Love and Responsibility*.

---

3. Karol Wojtyła, *Love and Responsibility*, trans. Grzegorz Ignatik (Boston: Pauline Books & Media, 2013).

4. For an extended discussion on the link between the Pope's papal and pre-papal writings, see Richard Spinello, *The Encyclicals of John Paul II: An Introduction and Commentary* (Lanham, MD: Rowman & Littlefield, 2012).

# Acknowledgments

This book owes much to the supportive environment for research and writing at Boston College. I also owe a debt to my colleagues and students at Saint John's Seminary in Boston with whom I have discussed some of the key ideas in this book. I would like to extend my thanks to the priests and parishioners at Saint Mary of the Assumption Parish in Dedham, Massachusetts, where Pope John Paul II is held in the highest esteem. I am indebted to our Youth Minister, J. P. Manning, for organizing a parish seminar on *Love and Responsibility*, and to those parishioners who attended and gave me such perceptive feedback. Also I would like to offer a special word of thanks to our pastor, Father William Kelly, and his assistant, Father Paul Sullivan.

My deepest gratitude goes to the editors at Pauline Books & Media for their professionalism, editorial skills, and astute suggestions. I am especially grateful to Christina M. Wegendt, FSP, for her confidence in my work and for her wise counsel and encouragement. Marianne Lorraine Trouvè, FSP, also deserves special mention; her insightful comments and deft editorial hand have improved almost every page.

Finally, I am especially indebted to my wife, Susan T. Brinton, for reading and editing the first draft of this book. Her constant encouragement and moral support have been immeasurably beneficial to me during the solitary hours spent writing three books on the late Holy Father's works. She first introduced me to the writings of John Paul II, and her passion for this subject matter matches my own. It is a great privilege to dedicate this book to her.

RICHARD A. SPINELLO

*Totus Tuus*

February 11, 2014

# Chapter 1

# Who Is Karol Wojtyła and
# Why Read *Love and Responsibility*?

## *(Author's Introductions, pp. xxi–xxviii)*[1]

## Karol Wojtyła and the philosophy of personalism

After his ordination to the priesthood, Karol Wojtyła's energies were absorbed with writing and speaking about the subject of romantic love between a man and a woman. His play *The Jeweler's Shop*, written in 1960 amid the social turbulence of post-war Poland, also dealt with this theme of marital intimacy. A character in the play remarks that "love is a constant challenge, thrown to us by God."[2]

---

1. This notation and those following other chapter headings refer to the corresponding sections in *Love and Responsibility*. This book does not treat the supplement on "Sexology and Ethics," and it does not explicitly consider the valuable essay "On the Meaning of Spousal Love," which was published separately in order to defend certain arguments in the original text. However, that essay is referred to on numerous occasions in the chapters ahead.

2. Karol Wojtyła, *The Jeweler's Shop*, in *The Collected Plays and Writings on Theater*, ed. B. Taborski (Berkeley: University of California Press, 1987), act 3, scene 5.

Those who come together as a "one-flesh" union overcome the existential loneliness of Adam before Eve's creation, but must confront many obstacles in this fallen world.

Wojtyła also taught popular courses on sexual ethics at the Catholic University of Lublin, where he occupied the Chair of Ethics from 1956 until his election to the papacy in 1978. During his tenure at the university Wojtyła developed his commitment to the philosophy of personalism. The whole Lublin faculty viewed its mission as a vocation to defend the special dignity of the human person against obstinate ideological opponents.[3] The chief opponent during the 1950s was atheistic Communism. But today personalism has many other enemies, such as materialism—a misguided philosophy that reduces the person to mere matter, a being determined in his actions by the imperatives of biology. Materialism continues to grow in popularity and has been called the new religion of modern man.[4] The essence of personalism, instead, is the conviction that the human person is not determined by history or biology and enjoys complete superiority over all other creatures. But the Lublin brand of personalism had a certain Thomistic and existential flavor. It emphasized the person as master of himself (*dominus sui*), with a spiritual center of activity able to shape his identity through the choices he makes.[5]

Wojtyła believed that the philosophy of personalism could help us discern the requirements and contours of marital love. But he was not just a philosophy professor who wrote about these matters from some secluded ivory tower. In a later memoir he described how young people had opened his eyes to the wonders of romantic love. Father Wojtyła said that when he was still a young priest he learned to love human love, and that became one of the fundamental themes of his priesthood. He knew that young people always seek the beauty in love, and they want to experience beautiful love. [6]

---

3. George Weigel, *Witness to Hope* (New York: HarperCollins, 1999), 131.

4. See John Searle, *Mind: A Brief Introduction* (Oxford: Oxford University Press, 2004), 48. Materialists deny the existence of the soul and tend to conceive the person as an animal with a sophisticated brain.

5. Saint Thomas Aquinas, *Summa Theologiae*, q. 6, art. 2, ad. 2.

6. Pope John Paul II, *Crossing the Threshold of Hope* (New York: Alfred Knopf, 1994), 123.

Some may see this as an odd interest, since Wojtyła himself was celibate, a man who could never enjoy romantic love with a woman. How could an unmarried man understand the sacrifices involved in married life, its daily trials, and its "constant challenge"? How could he possibly know anything about the meaning of sexual love or the romantic life of married couples? Wojtyła insisted that this lack of direct personal experience was not a hindrance, because priests have a rich indirect experience in this area derived from their extensive pastoral work. In that work they encounter a wide variety of situations that enriches their experience. Wojtyła spent a good deal of time with young married couples, encouraging them and instructing them about the faith. He recognized that marriage and family life are the primary road to happiness and fulfillment for most people. He firmly believed that the family is a communion of love and the pathway for the Church.[7] Yet at that time an understandable cynicism existed in Poland about all social institutions, including marriage. Beyond Poland, marriage was endangered by the rising ethos of individualism. In his writings and pastoral ministry, Wojtyła was anxious to demonstrate that marriage was neither a decaying institution nor one that was ready to be refashioned, no matter how some individuals were conducting their romantic lives.

Karol Wojtyła certainly had the practical experience and intellectual background to make the case for a traditional understanding of marriage and conjugal love. He was ordained to the priesthood at Wawel Cathedral in Kraków in 1946, and immediately went to Rome to pursue doctoral studies in philosophy at the Angelicum. Father Wojtyła studied under the famous Thomist philosopher, Father Reginald Garrigou-Lagrange, who was also a professor of spiritual theology. Wojtyła wrote his dissertation on Saint John of the Cross, a powerful mystic who became the inspiration for his understanding of spousal love as mutual and total self-giving. Shortly after returning to Poland in 1948, Father Wojtyła was assigned to begin a student chaplaincy at Saint Florian's Church near Kraków's Old Town. At this parish he held conferences for students, conducted retreats, and

---

7. Pope John Paul II, *Letter to Families* (Boston: St. Paul Books & Media, 1994), §2.

instituted marriage preparation courses for engaged couples. All of that was a novelty at the time. In his popular retreats he spoke often about marital love and about how sexual desire cannot be severed from charity and mutual self-donation.[8]

## The origins and purpose of the book

*Love and Responsibility* gestated during those happy years when he worked as a parish priest at Saint Florian's and later as a teacher at Lublin. The book is based on some of the lectures he delivered at the university as part of a comprehensive course on ethics. Several years prior to its publication, Father Wojtyła took a group of university students to the Mazurian Lakes district of northeastern Poland. There he circulated drafts of his manuscript among his eager students. Early each morning, as the mist still shrouded the lakes, one member of the group would be assigned to read material on a particular topic, such as spousal love or chastity. That student would diligently work throughout the day on his or her presentation, and the whole group would assemble in the evening for a lively discussion on this topic. Wojtyła hoped to ensure that his arguments were not only logically sound but also resonated with a young audience. This is no surprise given the complexity of the topic and the difficulty of expressing these issues in practical terms.[9]

In 1958 Father Wojtyła was appointed auxiliary bishop of Kraków to assist Archbishop Bazniak. However, he still remained committed to working with young married couples. During his episcopal visits to different parishes in the diocese, he blessed many married couples and their families. He described this experience as one that touches the bond of the human community, which is shaped in the Church and which in turn helps to shape the Church.[10]

Two years after Wojtyła's ordination to the episcopacy, the original edition of *Love and Responsibility* appeared in Polish. This publication

8. Adam Boniecki (ed.), *Kalendarium of the Life of Karol Wojtyła* (Stockbridge, MA: Marian Press, 2000), 125.

9. See Weigel, *Witness to Hope*, 139–140.

10. Boniecki, *Kalendarium*, 196.

was not prepared by a major European publishing house but by the obscure Academic Society of the Catholic University of Lublin. The original version was quickly succeeded in 1962 by a revised and expanded edition, published by the more prestigious Znak publishing house. The final and definitive Polish edition was published in 2001.

The original publication of *Love and Responsibility* coincided with a time of great anticipation in the Catholic Church, which was eagerly awaiting the Second Vatican Council (1962–1965) called by Pope John XXIII. The Council recommended a renewal of moral theology, but it addressed the issues of marriage and sexual morality only briefly in documents such as *Gaudium et Spes*. The Council Fathers deferred discussion on one of the most contentious issues at the time, which was contraception. They directed that a special commission be set up to deal with this issue, which Pope Paul VI finally resolved in his 1968 encyclical, *Humanae Vitae*. Wojtyła's conclusions in *Love and Responsibility* anticipated the Pope's claim that the marital act must always retain its intrinsic connection to the procreation of human life.[11]

When Wojtyła published his book, the sexual revolution of the 1960s was on the horizon. This ferment would radically transform the cultural landscape and challenge the book's fundamental ideas. In 1960 no one would have predicted the scope and breadth of that "revolution," which continues to evolve in unpredictable fashion at the hands of various progressive ideologies. Its bitter fruits have been rampant promiscuity, abortion, divorce, same-sex marriage, widespread pornography, an escalating tolerance for polyamory (multiple sexual relationships), and a burgeoning hookup culture on college campuses. Even gender has become "flexible," no longer considered as an integral aspect of our embodied personhood, but something to be chosen or altered at will.

Wojtyła had not yet come to public notice in the early 1960s. This changed to some degree at the Second Vatican Council, which he attended as part of the Polish delegation. He had not traveled outside of Poland since his student days in Rome, so he relished the opportunity to take part in the Council sessions and to meet other bishops and

---

11. Pope Paul VI, "Humanae Vitae," *Acta Apostolicae Sedis* 60 (1968), par. 11.

theologians from around the world. The Polish bishops had a hand in crafting one of the Council's major documents, *Gaudium et Spes*, which lays out an anthropological vision similar to what we find in the opening pages of *Love and Responsibility*. It was also during the Council that Wojtyła was named Archbishop of Kraków.

Although Wojtyła's reputation had grown in both Poland and the wider Church, *Love and Responsibility* received only limited attention. It was soon translated into French, Italian, and Spanish, but interest in all of Wojtyła's writings languished until he was elected to the papacy in 1978. *Love and Responsibility* finally appeared in English in 1981. Despite this translation and the book's wider dissemination, it continues to be overshadowed by John Paul II's immensely popular work on the theology of the body.

Both works are complementary, of course, and together they serve to illustrate the intimate cooperation of faith and reason. While *Man and Woman He Created Them* is a theological work, *Love and Responsibility* has a "philosophical character," so it seeks to persuade through human reason rather than rely exclusively on the dogmas of faith (p. xxii). However, even some of Wojtyła's most ardent supporters misconstrue the aim of this work. According to George Hunston Williams, for example, *Love and Responsibility* is a book composed almost exclusively for Catholic young people, especially those who are in love and aspire to be married.[12] On the contrary, this book is intended to appeal to a much broader audience than Catholic youth. Wojtyła sought to rely on reasoned reflection as a way of putting Catholic sexual doctrine on a firm intellectual foundation. If that foundation is secure, it is quite possible to develop a well-grounded sexual ethic that is universal in its appeal rather than unique to Catholic teaching. This is a book for *all* young people and for anyone else anxious to learn about the nature of love and about moral ideals like marital fidelity and chastity.

Obviously, Wojtyła's book has a special appeal to reflective Catholics because it gives them reasoned arguments for the Church's teachings on human sexuality, which are enunciated in a small number of Scripture

---

12. George Hunston Williams, *The Mind of John Paul II* (New York: Seabury Press, 1981), 154.

passages, such as Mark 10:1–12 and Matthew 19:1–13. Wojtyła believed that it was not enough to just stipulate the norms that forbid certain behaviors, but it was also essential "to substantiate, interpret, and explain" (p. xxii). His hope was that people would more freely follow Jesus's teaching once they appreciated its logic and wisdom. By coming to know that the moral norms governing sexual behavior protect the dignity of the person and contribute to human flourishing, those norms cease to be perceived as a burden that constrains our freedom. As Wojtyła explains later in the book, it is not enough for man to restrain errant sexual desires, he "must know 'why' he restrains them" (p. 183).

In his revised Introduction, the Pope explains that these Gospel texts on conjugal morality provide an "incentive for philosophical reflection" (p. xxvi). He is indirectly affirming the unity of truth, whether it comes from the light of Revelation or reason. If the statements of Jesus bear the mark of truth, which they must, we are inspired to discern the rational arguments that support these ethical truths. Those arguments, which reflect an immutable moral order, can be a bulwark against the ethical falsehoods and prejudices of secular humanism. Honest, rational inquiry confirms the moral truths enunciated in Sacred Scripture about the sanctity of life, sexual complementarity, and the indissolubility of marriage.

Thus, *Love and Responsibility* is really a work of philosophical theology, since it draws from both sources to bear witness to the truth about human sexual morality. Wojtyła certainly believed that in Sacred Scripture God revealed a natural pattern for human sexuality, but this book is primarily a treatise on ethics, a rational justification that must stand or fall on its own philosophical merits. Like any philosophical endeavor, it relies on a disciplined method, precise logical reasoning, and careful distinctions to expose the universal meaning of love and human sexuality.

## Importance of *Love and Responsibility*

No philosophy book is easy to read and this one is surely no exception. As a result, many people are put off by the challenge of grappling with such a demanding work. But the benign neglect of this extraordinary book is unfortunate. Wojtyła's treatise is a magisterial and intriguing attempt to define a sexual ethic focused on the dignity of the whole embodied human person. While other books have plowed similar furrows, few have the intellectual coherence, reverberating subtleties, and sensitivity found in *Love and Responsibility*. For many decades Catholic sexual morality was captive to the so-called "manualist" approach. Moral theology was taught from manuals based on legal and canonical authorities, and it seemed to be only remotely related to Sacred Scripture. This focus on moral laws and exceptions to those laws appeared to separate the virtue of love from sexual love, leaving the latter in a confounding obscurity. As Wojtyła explained, it is necessary to bring about the "introduction of love into love," to reintegrate sexual and romantic love with the virtue of charity (p. xxiii). Marital love should always be a delicate blending of *eros* and *agape*. Wojtyła's clear insight and originality in accomplishing this task is deftly combined with his supple awareness of sensuality's positive power, provided it is integrated through reason. The result is a fluent and provocative book, well ahead of its time and yet deeply enriched by the resources of the ancient Catholic tradition.

Those scholars who have read and studied Wojtyła's work recognize both its philosophical strengths as well as its potential pedagogic impact. Many theologians have effusively praised the book over the years. John Grondelski considers it to be a masterful work, while Janet Smith believes that *Love and Responsibility* belongs on the list of Great Books of the Western World. She predicts that many generations to come will read this book and ponder what it has to say about human relationships.[13] Moral theologian William May also acclaims the book as a "profound" work of moral reasoning that prepares the way for the theology of the body.[14] Philosophers like John Crosby have relied heavily on this work to develop their own personalist approach to sexual morality.

---

13. Janet Smith, "John Paul II and *Humanae Vitae*," in *Why Humanae Vitae Was Right*, ed. Janet Smith (San Francisco: Ignatius Press, 1993), 232. John Grondelski, "The Fiftieth Anniversary of *Love and Responsibility*: An Appreciation," *FCS Quarterly* Winter (2010): 25–29.

14. William May, *Theology of the Body in Context: Genesis and Growth* (Boston: Pauline Books & Media, 2010), 3.

Crosby believes that Wojtyła was given a rare and special gift for understanding the dynamic of conjugal love.[15] Even the eminent theologian Father Henri De Lubac, S.J., was quick to defend the book when it was criticized in the 1960s for its audacity and frankness. In his Preface to the French edition, De Lubac writes that Wojtyła's treatment of sexual ethics stands out for his careful analysis and rigorous thought, along with his concern to integrate these problems and all their aspects into an overall vision of human reality.[16]

Why do these noted philosophers and theologians esteem this book so highly? They appreciate *Love and Responsibility's* eloquence and carefully woven arguments, meant to persuade even the most cynical minds that the unleashing of our sexual desires is not the path to authentic human flourishing. These philosophical arguments, though not complex, follow a logical structure that shapes the entire book. Wojtyła first describes the nature of the human person. He then presents and defends a primary ethical principle consistent with that nature, which he calls the "personalistic norm." On this stable foundation, he constructs a theory of sexual morality that is difficult to dismiss if we are sincere about fostering a moral outlook that respects our bodily personhood. The whole purpose of the book is to demonstrate how one person can relate to another person in a sexual manner without using or mistreating that person as a mere object of pleasure. Wojtyła shifts the axis of discussion about sexual issues away from a legalistic perspective and toward the person, who is the radiating center of love and responsibility. While sensitive to the discoveries of modern science, he refuses to let psychology and medicine have the last word on these issues because "sexual ethics is a domain of the person" (p. xxiv).

Contrary to popular wisdom, few contemporary philosophical works deal with the issues of sex or sexual politics. While a consensus is emerging in universities and other cultural institutions about the moral suitability of extramarital sexual relations or homosexual activity, there

---

15. John Crosby, "Karol Wojtyła's Personalist Understanding of Man and Woman," in *Personalist Papers* (Washington, D.C.: Catholic University of America Press, 2004), 244.

16. That preface has been reprinted in Henri De Lubac, S.J., *Theology in History* (San Francisco: Ignatius Press, 1996), 581.

is no single, prominent theory of sexual ethics that justifies those beliefs. As G. J. McAleer observes, although Plato reflected on this theme, we cannot find a major twentieth-century philosopher, like a Martin Heidegger or a Ludwig Wittgenstein, who has crafted a comprehensive sexual ethic.[17] Perhaps a notable exception is the distinguished work of Dietrich von Hildebrand, whose treatise, called *The Nature of Love*, has recently been translated into English. Like von Hildebrand, Karol Wojtyła has thought and written extensively on this issue in order to develop a theory of sexual morality that has continuing relevance for current debates about contraception, reproductive technology, and redefining the nature of marriage. We know that Wojtyła/John Paul II fully supported the Catholic Church's clear norms on sexual morality. However, he was not content to rely only on Revelation, even though it allows us to formulate "quite clear views on the given topic" (p. xxii). Rather, he also wanted to employ wise moral arguments, easily grasped by our natural human intelligence, to confirm these norms as the basis for a common understanding of sexual morality that does not depend solely on religious beliefs.

The need for this book is far more urgent now than when it first appeared over fifty years ago. Since the 1960s, when the sexual revolution began sweeping across the world, absolute sexual freedom and unlimited autonomy has become a surrogate for acceptable sexual behavior. The appeal of subversive doctrines such as "free love" or "love without responsibility" is not hard to understand. In addition, there is widespread misapprehension about sexuality and the true nature of human love. For decades young men and women have been taught that casual sex is morally permissible and even a liberating experience that satisfies the longings of one's "inner self." As a result, many people do not know what romantic love is anymore. Its meaning has been gradually submerged by perverted cultural symbols and progressive attitudes. Love is often equated with sensuality and the rhapsodic delights of emotional attachment. This stereotype is popularized every day in

---

17. G.J. McAleer, *Ecstatic Morality and Sexual Politics* (New York: Fordham University Press, 2005), xiii–xiv.

popular television shows and movies. Many people, including Catholics, fail to grasp that the marital act must be a full bodily gift of self to one's spouse in order to consummate a real personal union. The once clear distinctions between love and lust, or between authentic sexual fulfillment and indulgence, seem to have become hopelessly obscured.

However, as the sexual revolution intensified, it became swiftly apparent that the promise of emancipation from the responsibilities of sexual behavior could never be fulfilled. While many have steadfastly refused to believe that this harmful moral transformation that reduces sex to recreation causes ill-effects, those effects have been well documented by sociologists like Mary Eberstad. She unmasks the dream of "carefree sex" as a chimera and presents empirical data showing that monogamous marriage is far better for a person's happiness and well-being than a series of casual sexual relationships.[18] The novelty of endless promiscuity is no match for the romantic stability of a sound marriage.

The sexual revolution, however, now manifest on college campuses in the form of the ubiquitous but dehumanizing "hookup" culture, has exposed many young adults to various pathologies including a rampant disregard for the well-being of women. In this permissive environment, saturated with alcohol and drug abuse, 19 percent of college women report that they have been the victims of some form of sexual assault.[19] Consensual hooking up, of course, is no substitute for a real relationship and can only lead to isolation and dissatisfaction. Moreover, the heralded birth control pill has not liberated women as once predicted, but has legitimized male promiscuity and exposed women to its devastating psychological effects.[20] Another consequence of this moral transformation is that cohabitation, casual sex, and divorce have destabilized marriage and family life.

---

18. Mary Eberstadt, *Adam and Eve after the Pill: Paradoxes of the Sexual Revolution* (San Francisco: Ignatius Press, 2012), 21–35.

19. Ibid., 79.

20. See Steven Rhoads, *Taking Sex Differences Seriously* (San Francisco: Encounter Books, 2004), 96–97.

Finally, the scourge of pornography, which relentlessly depersonalizes both men and women, continues unabated thanks to the encroachment of the Internet and other technologies, which make this material so readily accessible even to young children.

The rise in reckless promiscuity and abortion that has accompanied the sexual revolution was boldly predicted in *Humanae Vitae*, which reaffirmed Catholic teaching on the impermissibility of contraception. That encyclical also warned that the deliberate sterilization of the sexual act would lower moral standards, reduce respect for women in society, and lead to an increase in marital infidelity. All of these predictions have been strikingly confirmed by ample sociological data.[21]

Before writing this prophetic encyclical, Pope Paul VI wanted input from moral theologians and Church leaders, and so he appointed a papal commission to study the matter. The author of *Love and Responsibility*, Bishop Wojtyła, was a logical choice for this commission, but he could not attend the meetings due to passport problems. Nonetheless, Wojtyła created a diocesan commission that issued its own report, "The Foundations of the Church's Doctrine on the Principles of Conjugal Life." These principles were based to a great extent on Wojtyła's reflections in *Love and Responsibility*, which are anchored in a personalist approach to conjugal morality. That report was sent on to Rome for the Pope's review. We are also told that Pope Paul VI was reading *Love and Responsibility* when he composed *Humanae Vitae,* and that he was profoundly influenced by Wojtyła's arguments.[22]

Although themes from the Kraków report and *Love and Responsibility* can be found in *Humanae Vitae*, the encyclical did not frame its primary arguments in a personalist context. The encyclical left no doubt that each marital act must be oriented to procreation, since the unitive and procreative dimensions of the marital act cannot be disconnected. However, Paul VI does not defend this proposition in

---

21. Eberstadt, *Adam and Eve after the Pill,* 136–137.

22. Paul Johnson, *Pope John Paul II and the Catholic Restoration* (Ann Arbor, MI: Servant Publications, 1981), 32–33. See also Janet Smith, "John Paul II and *Humanae Vitae*," 232–233.

personalist terms, preferring instead to emphasize that such teachings are deeply rooted in Revelation. Arguably, this deficiency in *Humanae Vitae* left the Church vulnerable to accusations that it was still bedeviled by the shadowy residue of Manichaeism and the denigration of sexuality.[23]

*Love and Responsibility*, especially when read in conjunction with *Man and Woman He Created Them: A Theology of the Body*, elucidates in personalistic terms why marriage can only be understood in terms of an unconditional sharing and total union at the bodily level that creates an intimate community centered on children.[24] It demonstrates that the sexual act must express that union based on reciprocal self-donation in order to preserve the generous character of love. Positive contraception, on the other hand, means that the conjugal act cannot express a loving personal union precisely because it is anti-unitive. Wojtyła's book also provides an inspiring and edifying vision of spousal love to those who have been deceived by the false promises offered by the radical feminists and elites, who have been in the forefront of reshaping our attitudes about human sexuality. Wojtyła unveils the universal meaning of conjugal love and dispels the idea that each culture can create its own moral universe by refashioning sexual ethics to suit its arbitrary desires. He directs convincing arguments against the thin intellectual framework of hedonistic utilitarianism, which proposes pleasure or satisfaction as the source of happiness. By reading this book and meditating on its more challenging passages, those who have been led astray by the ideological myths and seductive arguments of our ambient culture can retrieve a proper understanding of conjugal love and sexuality through the lens of personalism.

However, aside from marriage, *Love and Responsibility* does not delve into specific issues or explicitly prescribe acceptable conduct compatible with the proper moral norms. It does not articulate easy formulas nor make any elaborate incursions into moral casuistry. Rather, this

---

23. Weigel, *Witness to Hope*, 209.

24. Alexander Pruss, *One Body: An Essay in Christian Sexual Ethics.* (South Bend, IN: University of Notre Dame Press, 2013), 146.

book "attempts to create an integral vision of the problem," recognizing that particular solutions can be deduced from that vision (p. xxviii).

Pope Paul VI made Bishop Wojtyła a cardinal in 1967. Despite his expanding duties in the Church, the young cardinal remained intensely interested in marriage preparation and family issues. The rapid development and dissemination of reproductive technologies was becoming a major concern. During a retreat given to the papal household in 1976, two years before his election to the papacy, Cardinal Wojtyła warned that the "man of progress" was becoming unjust to his Creator.[25] To those in the audience who had read *Love and Responsibility*, these would have been very familiar words. We can only restore that justice in the sexual sphere by rediscovering the natural meaning and purpose of human sexuality as the provident Creator designed it.

---

25. Karol Wojtyła, *Sign of Contradiction* (New York: Seabury Press, 1979), 33.

# Chapter 2

# The Human Person

## *(Chapter I: Part One)*

As a book about ethics, *Love and Responsibility* addresses questions such as: "What must I do?" or "How should I live?" In general, we must pursue what is good for ourselves and for others. Basic human goods worthy of our choices include life and health along with marriage, friendship, and worship of God. But this question about the good cannot be satisfactorily answered unless we understand the nature of this "I" who seeks out these goods. The anthropological question, "Who is man?" must logically precede any discussion of morality. It stands to reason that we cannot determine what is good for the human person unless we come to terms with his nature and how that nature is fulfilled.

Hence the opening chapter of *Love and Responsibility* addresses this vital theme of anthropology and serves as a foundation for the ethical analysis that follows. Wojtyła realizes that mistakes about the nature of the person can easily lead to flawed ethical judgments. The misconception that the person is a disembodied self just using a body has produced enormous confusion in the area of sexual morality. A person who experiences same-sex attractions, for example, might argue that a person's body and its gender is irrelevant when it comes to engaging in sexual relations with another individual. "It doesn't matter what we do with our bodies," he might say, "so long as we care about each other and respect everyone's freedom." At the same time, it is wrong to endorse the now popular materialist view that the person is just a body without a spiritual soul, because this notion fails to esteem man highly enough. It fails to account for his spiritual capabilities, such as his capacity for conceptual thinking. If man is only a physical body with limited horizons, perhaps transient sexual pleasure is a worthy aspiration.

## The value of the person

However, unlike many of the materialists and secularists who want to topple the human person from his pedestal, Wojtyła argues for each person's intrinsic worth and supreme value. Moral theologians point to the biblical notion of man made in God's image as the source of man's dignity. As we first learn in Genesis, each person bears within himself the image of his Creator (Gn 1:26–27). Wojtyła does not elaborate on this biblical witness to man's dignity in this context, although he enthusiastically endorses the doctrine of man as *imago Dei* in many of his other writings. Rather, in keeping with the "philosophical character" of this work, he pursues a more logical approach based on the insights of natural reason rather than revelation.

Wojtyła accepts the premise that all human beings belong to the same species and therefore share in a basic equality. If we were not all essentially alike we couldn't talk about our "humanity," and it wouldn't even make sense to say that Jesus Christ assumed a human nature. This common humanity makes possible a common morality instead of a situation ethics, where each situation supplies its own "norm of action" (p. 101). However, while species membership is important for our basic equality, it is inadequate to account for the moral dignity and the exceptional qualities of the human person. "It is not sufficient," writes Wojtyła, "to speak of man as an individual of the species *Homo sapiens*" (p. 4).

The term "person" signifies that there is something more to man than belonging to a species, that there is "some particular fullness and perfection of being" (p. 4). In his essay "On the Meaning of Spousal Love," Wojtyła has explained that the person is uniquely gifted with self-possession. This self-possession, which becomes evident in the examination of human experience, is expressed in two ways. First, the person is aware of himself; only a person can utter the word "I" and know that it refers to him. Thus, a person possesses himself because he is present to himself from within by being conscious of himself and his actions. When Joe decides to feed the cat in the morning, he is aware of himself carrying out this simple action, and he can remember later in the day that he made this choice. Second, a person "possesses himself and determines himself" because he has mastery or control over his actions (p. 280). This power of self-determination, which is actualized by the will, is "based on reflection, and manifested in the fact that, while acting, man chooses what he wants to do" (p. 6). Only a person can envision something as a good or an objective (such as recovering one's health), know what he is doing in pursuing that good, and voluntarily choose to take the necessary steps (going to the doctor, taking medicine, etc.) to achieve that good.[1]

Unlike animals, a person enjoys self-possession because of his or her rational nature. The person possesses reason, so she is a rational being, which "by no means can be stated about any other being of the visible world" (p. 4). And man is such a being by virtue of his spiritual soul, which is "substantially united to the body" from the time of conception (p. 39). Our own experience confirms that only human beings have an intellect and will thanks to the soul, because only a human being is capable of thinking and making choices. Persons have an interior life and so differ from animals, which operate by instincts proper to their species. This "inner life" revolves around truth and goodness. We can know the truth through our intellect and choose what is good through the will. It is because of this rich inner life or "interiority" that man is a person.

Thanks to their being as embodied spirits, human beings have a unique prerogative that makes possible distinctive qualities such as conceptual thought and freedom. Since a person has freedom we can hold

---

1. See John Finnis, *Intention and Identity,* Collected Essays: Volume II (Oxford: Oxford University Press, 2011), 133–151.

that person morally accountable for his or her actions. Thus, not only do we belong to the same human species, that species consists of human persons, so each of us is a *somebody* rather than a *something*.

## The person is incommunicable

The dignity that we possess as persons with a rational nature is a dignity common to all human beings, who share in this common humanity. But Wojtyła wants to argue for another source of dignity that comes from our existential uniqueness and our remarkable originality. Although we all have this rational nature in common, we are not all the same. Each person is unique and unrepeatable, and exists only once. At the heart of this uniqueness is the reality that each person is incommunicable and inalienable. This means that a person belongs to herself and to no one else. Each person is a self-possessing and independent being. A person does not "share" her inner life with another, even though she does participate in the same common humanity. That inner life is full of thoughts, dreams, and aspirations that make every individual so unique and mysterious. Moreover, thanks to his will and reasoning power, each person realizes that he is his own property, though he is always "a possession of the Creator" (p. 235). Self-possession and self-governance does not nullify our created status nor does it "*abolish* the supreme *authority of the Creator*" over the human person (p. 281)

This reality of self-possession is confirmed in the experience that no one can understand for me and no one else can will or want in my place, for no one else can "substitute his act of the will for mine" (p. 6). An example might help us understand what Wojtyła is suggesting. Through flattery, generous gifts, and the promise of a luxurious lifestyle, a man might try to persuade a woman to love him and to be his wife. Perhaps his coaxing finally works and this woman does end up marrying him not because she loves him, but because his vast wealth gives her comfort and security. She often tells her new husband that she loves him, because she knows that these declarations of love will make him happy. However, this man can't force his new wife to actually love him and to truly want him as her spouse. No matter what she says to him, in her inner life the woman doesn't really love her wealthy husband and doesn't prefer him as her spouse, and no external pressure can change her mind. Within the depths of her privacy and interiority, where her personal self serenely dwells, this woman is "incommunicable" and untouchable. She is beyond the reach of external forces.

The first couple we meet in *The Jeweler's Shop*, Andrew and Theresa, seem keenly aware of the possibility that this "incommunicability" can form a barrier between people. Andrew describes Theresa as a "whole world, just as distant as any other man, as any other woman." And yet, he explains, something about her "allowed me to think of throwing a footbridge." Andrew's attraction and growing love for Theresa enabled him to throw that "footbridge," which rescued him from Adam-like solitude. Through the eyes of love, the enigmatic depths of Theresa begin to be revealed to him as she shares her innermost thoughts and dreams with the man she trusts and loves.[2]

Like Andrew, we know that each person is a "whole world" unto himself. That person is his own master because he exists for his own sake and does not "belong" to another. Because of these features, particularly the innate independence that comes to us by way of our interiority, each person deserves the opportunity to act independently and choose freely in his or her moral life. Each person should have the freedom and moral independence to choose her own reasonable ends proper to her nature based on her particular desires and aspirations. We must respect that freedom up to the point where a person makes evil choices; under these conditions, it is morally permissible to interfere with another's freedom to try to prevent him or her from harming oneself or harming others. This moral independence or liberty, says Wojtyła, is essential for human relationships and serves as the principal basis of human culture and education. It is hard to imagine a culture worthy of the person that does not respect human longing for truth, freedom, and dignity.

---

2. Karol Wojtyła, *The Jeweler's Shop*, Act 1, Scene 1.

# The person is an embodied spirit

Given the spiritual qualities of the person, it may be tempting to reduce the person to his or her spiritual nature and conceive the body as only ancillary to personhood. But throughout *Love and Responsibility* and in all his other writings, Wojtyła has rejected any form of dualism that separates body and soul into two distinct substances, uneasily joined in human life. Rather, he affirms that "the human person . . . 'is a body'"; he is not a spiritual self using a body as if it were an instrument (p. 5). More precisely, the person is an embodied spirit. This means that body and soul are two complementary factors "constituting one personal being, which owes its [specific nature] precisely to the spiritual soul" (p. 20). The soul carries out both the operations of the body and its own higher spiritual operations that go beyond the mediation of the senses. This strong emphasis on the person's wholeness, consistent with the teaching of Saint Thomas Aquinas and the entire Catholic intellectual tradition, has significant implications for sexual ethics since love is always expressed and mediated through the body.[3] We live out our moral lives as embodied persons, and this means that the body is not just raw material to be manipulated by the spiritual self, but an integral part of our personhood. Therefore we can never disregard the personal dignity of the human body nor its role as an anticipatory sign of self-giving.[4]

Finally, although he does not discuss this matter in the early part of the book, Wojtyła repeatedly insists that this embodied person is not by nature solitary and self-sufficient. Rather, since each person is a "social being," he or she finds fulfillment in communion with others (p. 34). There is no authentic "I" without a "we." This interpersonal communion, such as a family or religious community, is created when persons

---

3. According to Saint Thomas, "Body and soul are not two actually existing substances; instead, one actually existing substance arises from both." *Summa contra Gentiles*, II, c.69. See also W. Norris Clarke, S.J., "Metaphysics as Mediator between Revelation and the Natural Sciences," *Communio* 28 (Fall 2001), pp. 464–487.

4. John Paul II explains this further in *Veritatis Splendor* (Boston: Pauline Books & Media, 1993), §48–49.

freely give themselves to others. Inscribed into the nature of personal being itself is "the potency and power of giving oneself, and this potency is closely joined with the structure of self-possession and self-governance proper to the person" (p. 281). Although man possesses himself, he is made for self-donation, and through self-donation he comes to possess himself, to be himself, more fully. In the essay on spousal love, Wojtyła refers to the "law of the gift": the person is made to give herself, and that gift of self becomes "indispensable *for the union of persons*" (p. 286). Central to Wojtyła's personalistic vision of sexuality is the fundamental idea that authentic self-fulfillment must be based on the mutual sharing and interpersonal communion made possible by love.

## Summary

Taken in summary, the first few pages of *Love and Responsibility* provide us with an insight into our human nature that opens the way for understanding the ethical character of human sexuality. Human beings share a common humanity, which ensures their equality. By virtue of the soul, each of us is also a "somebody," a person gifted with self-possession. The person's spiritual or rational nature elevates him above all other creatures because his rational powers make him superior to those creatures. The soul is the foundation of our intrinsic worth or human dignity. The reality of human dignity must be recognized for every member of the human species and cannot be nullified for any reason. The soul makes possible self-governance and opens up the possibilities of a complex inner life. Each person, who is the master of himself, is unique and incommunicable such that he belongs to himself and to no one else. Finally, the person is a body, but a body of a special kind thanks to its spiritual soul. This embodied person achieves self-fulfillment through self-donation, which lifts man out of his solitude and into intimate solidarity and communion with others. The person is made for a simple purpose: to love and to be loved.

It is only by restoring the person to her rightful place in creation, recognizing her exceptional qualities, that we can begin to retrieve the original meaning of human sexuality expressed so compellingly in the Book of Genesis. And it is only by acknowledging the body's inherent dignity and personal meaning that we can appreciate why sexually deviant behavior that often justifies itself by separating the body from the person defies human nature and reorients the sexual act away from generosity. We need this solid idea of what the human person is to discover the truth about human sexuality.

# Chapter 3

# The Personalistic Norm

## *(Chapter I: Part One)*

Now that we know who we are, we can begin to decipher our moral obligations. As persons, we consciously initiate actions to achieve a certain goal. Often we use different things or objects to achieve that goal. For example, we might use wood and stone to build a house in order to secure adequate shelter, or use fossil fuels to provide energy for a vehicle. "Man in his diverse activity," explains Wojtyła, "makes use of the whole created world" and "takes advantage of its resources" for the goals that he sets (p. 8). Sometimes, of course, our actions involve other people, and we can also be on the receiving end of such actions. In Wojtyła's terminology, persons are subjects or moral agents, and they can also be moral patients when they are the object of another person's action. If Jill hires Steven to work in her shop as a sales clerk, she is the subject and he is the "patient" or object. But how is it possible for a person to be the object of another person's action without using or mistreating that person? How can Jill manage her new employee without treating him as if he were just another "resource," as a *something* rather than a *somebody*?

# To love or to use

The key question in ethics, therefore, is this: What should be the guiding moral principle when our actions are directed at other people? Wojtyła believes that we can adopt one of two basic moral attitudes: love or use. We can choose to use another person as we commonly use other things around us, as instruments or tools. To use, he explains, means to "employ some object of action as a means to an end" (p. 7). People use others in many ways, but especially when they are coercive or deceptive. The stockbroker who lies to the widow in order to get a big commission on a worthless stock is shamelessly using her merely as a means to acquire wealth for himself. He doesn't care about the widow's worthy end of financial security. In such cases we treat people as we would other things, as pawns to be manipulated for our own self-serving designs. The alternative is to treat other persons with love, with the benevolence and loving-kindness they deserve as persons.

To manipulate another person through such tactics as lying and coercion cannot be morally justified. Deception and coercion violate a person's freedom and moral independence. They block a person from choosing an end or good he would have chosen had he not been the victim of coercion or deception. Each person is an end in herself and exists for her own sake, not for the sake of another. The widow exists for herself, to pursue her own fulfillment, and should not be an instrumental means for making the stockbroker wealthy. "A person should not be merely a means to an end for another person," writes Wojtyła. "This is excluded due to the very nature of the person, due to what every person simply is" (pp. 9–10).

Thus, this moral principle forbidding the use of another as a mere instrument is grounded firmly in Wojtyła's view of the person. Thanks to the soul, a person is a thinking and willing subject, an independent center of moral acts, who can choose his or her own ends and objectives. According to Wojtyła, "every person is capable by his nature to define his ends himself" (p. 10). Of course, a person's ends or goals must be good and reasonable, always proper to our human nature. When we reject this capability of free choice or self-governance in someone else and treat a person merely as a means to advance our own selfish ends, we violate that person in his "very essence" (p. 10). On the contrary, we must recognize the significance of purposeful actions and choices, because they define and shape our character.

In life every person makes countless choices, both big and small. A person chooses a certain profession or a religious vocation, marriage, or single life, where to go to college, and where to live. But if someone blocks or disrupts another person's choices for her own advantage, she exploits that person because she is unwilling to let him exist for his own sake. The most odious form of such exploitation is slavery, which makes the other person an extension of his owner and denies him any independence or any opportunity to be his own master and to control his own destiny. Theologians like Romano Guardini have explained the obvious conflict between being a person and being owned by someone else.[1]

The immorality of using others is further shown by the fact that even God respects our moral independence. God has made us with a certain nature, ordered to basic human goods that fulfill us. He allows us to come to know and value these goods or ends. But decisions about which goods to strive for (such as marriage or the priesthood) and the means to be used to attain such goods depend on our own free will. In this we are guided by reason and supported by intellectual virtues such as prudence. God does not even save a person against his or her will. Rather, "God lets man know the supernatural end, but the decision to strive for this end, its choice, is left to man's freedom" (p. 11).

## The personalistic norm

Wojtyła refers to this master moral principle that forbids using another person instrumentally as the personalistic norm. According to this universal moral standard, rather than regard other persons as mere objects to be used for our own selfish ends, we must always respect their morally reasonable, self-chosen ends. When persons are treated in such

---

1. Romano Guardini, *The World and the Person* (Chicago: Henry Regnery, 1965), 103–131. See also John Crosby's treatment of these issues in *The Selfhood of the Human Person* (Washington, D.C.: Catholic University of America Press, 1996), 9–25.

a way, the natural order "acquires personalistic properties," because the person is elevated above other beings and the personal qualities of rationality and freedom are suitably respected in human actions (p. 11).

This ethical impulse to treat the other as an end seems fundamental for promoting basic human justice. If Jill decides she wants to marry Bill and this is a reasonable choice (that is, she is a mature woman, Bill is a decent man, etc.), her family and friends must respect her choice. Jill's father may want her to marry Carl because he is quite wealthy and generous, and the father believes he will benefit from Carl's largesse. But Jill doesn't love Carl, and any attempt by her father to entice her into that marriage is unjust, because it is equivalent to using her for his own self-serving purposes.

This moral standard has a distinguished pedigree in the history of moral philosophy. It was first presented by the German philosopher Immanuel Kant as the second version of his categorical imperative, which he also called the Formula of Humanity: "Act so that you treat humanity, whether in your own person or in that of another, always as an end and never as a means only."[2] In *Crossing the Threshold of Hope* John Paul II explained that by using the personalistic principle he was seeking to translate the evangelical commandment of love into the terminology of philosophical ethics.[3] For Kant, this principle is the supreme limiting condition on the way we behave toward others because it protects the dignity of the person.[4] The same thing could surely be said for Karol Wojtyła. Even actions that seem to bring about good results cannot be undertaken if they involve the degrading use of another person as a mere instrument. From the personalistic norm we can deduce actions that can never be done (such as taking the life of an innocent person) along with positive duties toward ourselves and our neighbors. These duties that flow from the personalistic norm can also be expressed in terms of rights that direct us to act in certain ways out of deference to the dignity of other persons.

---

2. Immanuel Kant, *Foundation of the Metaphysics of Morals*, trans. L. Beck (Indianapolis: Bobbs-Merrill, 1959), 54.

3. See Pope John Paul II, *Crossing the Threshold of Hope*, 200–201.

4. Kant, *Foundation of the Metaphysics of Morals*, 64.

How is it possible to overcome a "consumer attitude" toward persons and avoid situations where one person becomes for another merely an object of use? To prevent that from happening, people who live or work together must assimilate the common good of their respective communities and make it their own. That common good forms a bond among people; it "unites the acting persons 'from within'" (p. 12). For example, the workplace always involves some danger that employers or managers will treat employees opportunistically. However, if everyone concentrates more intently on the common good of efficiently producing products and serving customers, that danger will be mitigated. Managers and employees will be united by an attitude of cooperation that is more equivalent to love than to using. If both groups strive for a valid common good that always includes the fair distribution of benefits, it is far less likely that the employee will be used merely as a "blind tool" (p. 13).

This credible supposition that the bond of a common good prevents relationships from drifting into selfish using also applies to marriage. In order to escape the trap of using one another, a married couple must focus on the "common end" of marriage: procreation, family, and the continual maturing of the marital relationship (p. 14). So long as a married couple subordinate themselves to this good, it is much less likely they will exploit each other. Concentration on that common good will enable an individual to overcome his self-interest (which leads to using others) and seek this larger purpose instead.

## Second type of use

The verb "to use" has another meaning, which has special significance for sexual morality. This area of morality concentrates on "reciprocal relations between persons of different sex" (p. 16). To use in this context means to enjoy or to experience pleasure, a pleasure that arises through both the sexual activity itself and the object of that activity, who is always another person. The person becomes the source of pleasure when he or she is a partner in sexual activity. In Wojtyła's view, this sort of pleasure can never be purely sensual, since it always has a connection with another person. Even an exclusively bodily love has an interpersonal dimension because it involves two persons. Unlike animals, man's sexual life takes place on a personal rather than instinctual level.

Nothing is wrong with pleasure itself when it accompanies the sexual act within the context of marriage. But a problem arises when a rational person isolates pleasure in a relationship and treats it as a "distinct end of action" (p. 17). If sexual relations with a person of the opposite sex are shaped only with this aim in view, that person is being used as a means for the sake of another's pleasure or enjoyment. A famous writer who claims to have been miserably married for many years once described his mistress as a "constant delight." His affair was no more than a temporary and convenient romance—there was great passion but no love, long-term commitment, or any real communion of persons. Such arrangements illustrate what Wojtyła is talking about: two people use each other's bodies as a source of sensual pleasure and emotional satisfaction.

This form of use is quite frequent, and it "can easily occur in the conduct" of both men and women (p. 17). Yet it cannot occur in the world of animals. For animals, sexual pleasure cannot be isolated as an end, so there is no possibility of "using." But things are different for the rational human person, whose intellect creates the opportunity for such manipulative behavior. Benevolence and the moral commitment of friendship, which orders our thoughts and feelings, make it plain that such using for pleasure cannot be condoned. In Wojtyła's words, "Only 'loving' excludes 'using,' also in that second meaning" (p. 18). We must carefully distinguish, however, between genuine solicitude for another person and the intention to use that person for pleasure, which can easily masquerade as love and concern.

This discussion on pleasure, rationality, and personhood begins to concentrate our attention on sexual love and sexual morality. Two issues are fundamental to sexual morality. The first involves the "finality" or primary purpose of the sexual life, which is always procreation (pp. 17–18). The second issue concerns the possibility that human beings can easily fall prey to being used by someone else as a source of pleasure, and use is the antithesis of love. As we will see, these two issues are closely interrelated. Sexual relations that have been deliberately sterilized or focused exclusively on pleasurable enjoyment fail to live up to the moral standard of conjugal love. But at this point, Wojtyła simply stresses that fidelity to the personalistic norm requires that any enjoyment of the other always be subordinate to the demands of love.

## Critique of utilitarianism

Wojtyła's apprehension about using other people extends into a pungent critique of the dangerous ethical theory known as utilitarianism. This popular philosophy has its roots in the work of the nineteenth-century British philosopher, Jeremy Bentham. It was given the name "consequentialism" by the distinguished Catholic philosopher, Elizabeth Anscombe. For Bentham, the highest moral imperative is to maximize happiness by bringing about the overall balance of pleasure over pain through our moral choices. Bentham equated happiness with pleasure and did not appear to differentiate higher pleasures from lower ones. Since the quantity of pleasure is equal, he once explained, the simple game of push-pin is every bit as good and worthwhile as poetry.[5] This sort of hedonistic utilitarianism was modified by later thinkers, but it becomes the focal point of Wojtyła's attention.

According to utilitarian logic, therefore, the right act is always the one that will optimize benefits over costs or pleasure over pain, in order to yield the greatest happiness for the greatest number of people. Utilitarianism, however, is based on a misguided anthropology that refuses to take into account the reality of man as a natural unity of body and soul. Together these create a "personal existence," whose specific nature flows from the soul. The utilitarian supposes that the person is endowed with the property of practical reason so that he can direct his activities to maximizing pleasure and minimizing pain or discomfort. This is the utilitarian's basic principle of morality, with the caveat that pleasure must be maximized for everyone affected by one's action.

Wojtyła worries about the impact of utilitarianism, which has regrettably become "a characteristic property of contemporary man's

---

5. Ross Harrison, *Bentham* (London: Routledge, 1983), 5. See also Michael Sandel, *Justice* (New York: Farrar, Straus and Giroux, 2009), 52.

mentality and his attitude toward life" (p. 19). People have always used others, but now they do so quite deliberately and even believe that they are acting justly. The utilitarian ethic has two grave problems. First, utilitarianism is based on a subjective notion of the good. Happiness understood as maximum pleasure is conceived as the highest good. But pleasure is not the highest good; in fact, pleasure is at best only an incidental or "accidental" good, something that "may occur when acting" (p. 20). Pleasure only accompanies the realization of real human goods (including marital intimacy). A life of pleasure and emotional satisfaction is not a fulfilling life; on the contrary, life is fulfilled by activities and the realization of goods such as friendship and knowledge. Unlike these goods, pleasure, how our lives feel from within, is a subjective and passive experience.

The pursuit of pleasure for its own sake, therefore, is not a fulfilling activity that leads to real happiness. Pleasure is no more than an agreeable sensation that *happens* to us and that varies from one person to another. In a sexual relationship a woman may find certain things quite pleasurable while a man does not. Pleasure is transitory and incidental; it can also take many perverse forms, such as sadistic or masochistic pleasure. Hence, for all these reasons, "undertaking to act for the sake of pleasure itself as the exclusive or highest end naturally clashes with the proper structure of human acts" (p. 20). These acts should always aim at an intelligible or worthwhile good such as health or friendship. Accordingly, since pleasure cannot qualify as an objective and fulfilling good, it cannot become the bond or common goal between two people.

The second problem with utilitarianism is that it inevitably leads to selfish egoism that can never overcome itself in favor of altruism. Once a person accepts maximizing pleasure as an ethical imperative, he attributes value to the other person's pleasure but only insofar as he himself is experiencing pleasure. His actions are always to some degree self-serving, since they are inevitably focused on his own pleasure or emotional satisfaction. When his pleasure ceases, the relationship will end since the good of pleasure is no longer being optimized. For example, Fred may derive pleasure purely from his sexual relations with Sally, but Sally's pleasure comes from Fred's company, especially at those glittering social events she likes to attend where she is the envy of her friends. So long as they are both satisfied, pleasure is maximized and they appear to be a "happy" couple. They may even have the "appearance of altruism," because each one is concerned about the other's pleasure (p. 22). But once Fred is no longer sexually fulfilled, once he tires of Sally, pleasure or happiness is not being maximized and the moral course of action (true to the principle of utilitarianism) is to terminate the relationship, even if Sally is still happy about being with Fred.

The only escape from the inevitable encroachment of egoism that accompanies utilitarian reasoning is to find an objective good that unites persons. "This objective common good," explains Wojtyła, "is the foundation of love, and the persons choosing this common good together at the same time subordinate themselves to it" (p. 22). Love is the unification of persons. Love can only be based on an objective and enduring good that these persons pursue together, not an individual and subjective good like pleasure. Marriage and friendship are examples of objective goods because they have many benefits that are obvious to any reasonable person. The mutual pursuit of such an objective good that contributes to each person's human flourishing liberates individuals from subjectivism and from the egoism it conceals. If people like Fred and Sally were really in love, they would not be fixated on their own pleasure or self-interest but on a good that transcends and unites them, such as parenthood and family. Love is the permanent unification of persons, but that unification cannot depend on the fleeting sensation of pleasure.

Is there no way out of egoism once "utilitarian presuppositions" are endorsed (p. 23)? What about the familiar argument that two people can mutually agree to "use" each other by giving each other pleasure, thereby harmonizing their interests? Despite this harmony and temporary union of emotions, egoism persists in such relationships. The only difference is that the man's and woman's egoisms will match each other and converge for their mutual advantage. But, as we have seen, the moment these interests fail to coincide, the harmony dissipates. In this type of relationship everything depends on what I get from someone else. This egoistic sentiment erodes true interpersonal communion, which is based on a selfless, permanent, and exclusive commitment to the other person. There is no love because the "objective good, which constitutes love, is missing" (p. 23). These insecure relationships lack any active concern for the other person, who "sinks" to the level of being used as a tool or instrument for the other. If I treat someone as a means in a relationship, I cannot help but see myself in the same light. The end result is a kind of mutual self-serving that is the very opposite of what it means to love and to be loved.

Wojtyła's skepticism of utilitarian reasoning affirms that the commandment to love is incompatible with the utilitarian attitude. In proposing pleasure as the highest good, utilitarianism breeds an egoism and partiality that is always hostile to love. Utilitarianism is also divisive because it does not put forth a set of truly objective human goods that can unite and fulfill people who strive for them. Marriage and family are stable and permanent goods that can be shared, but pleasure is unstable, transitory, and cannot be shared.

## Love and the personalistic norm

The only morally suitable attitude toward the person is one that always affirms a person for his or her own sake and never permits the mere use of another for any reason, including pleasure. This attitude is expressed in the personalistic norm, which proposes a way of relating to another person that is in harmony with that person's intellectual nature and freedom. The personalistic norm recognizes that the person is to be valued higher than objects, as a being whose capacity for self-governance and spirituality deserves the highest respect. Unlike the principle of utility, this principle does justice to the reality of personhood. The personalistic norm has been formulated negatively since it states that the person is the type of being who is incompatible with being used by others. But a positive formulation is also possible: "the person is a kind of good to which only love constitutes the proper and fully-mature relation" (p. 25). Strictly speaking, the Gospel commandment to love should not be identified with the personalistic norm. However, this universal norm substantiates the Gospel proclamation about love, and so there is a profound connection.

It logically follows that one who abides by this norm will treat the other with fairness, which will always take precedence over mere utility. Fairness implicates justice, giving the other what is due to him. And it is rightfully due to a person "to be treated as an object of love, and not as an object of use" (p. 26). Whoever loves a person is just to that person, but love cannot be reduced to justice. The personalistic norm represents the interpenetration of love and justice. The notion of love needs more elaboration, but it always consists in affirming the "supra-utilitarian" value of the person as a being who is never to be selfishly used by others (p. 27).

If this norm is to be preserved in the area of sexual relationships, we must carefully discern the proper conditions of erotic love that ensure that the persons involved are treated justly. This is a formidable challenge because in the sexual context what may appear as love sometimes represents a pattern of injustice. In sexual affairs, there is a "natural gravitation toward pleasure" (p. 27). It is easy to move from the experience of pleasure to the quest for pleasure for its own sake, so that mutual sexual satisfaction becomes normative. But when pleasure-seeking controls a romantic relationship, it can only end in tragic failure.

The task for sexual morality is to determine how sexual union can express intimate mutuality and generosity without the encroachment of a utilitarian attitude or egoism. To accomplish this task, the nature of love must be further clarified, but one thing is crystal clear: the love espoused in the Gospel can only be linked to the personalistic norm and never to utilitarian values. According to Wojtyła, it is always "within the scope of the personalistic norm" that appropriate solutions to sexual morality must be sought, if they are to be consistent with Christian morality (p. 28). This norm has universal validity, because it represents the only reasonable way to do justice to the person. So we might add that this norm can also serve as the foundation for a sexual morality that will have the same universal force.

## SUMMARY

Following the example of philosophers like Immanuel Kant, Wojtyła has proposed that personhood must be respected in all human actions, because every person has the capacity to "define his ends himself" (p. 10). Wojtyła calls this principle the personalistic norm, which prohibits using another person merely as a means for my own selfish needs instead of respecting that person's morally reasonable self-chosen ends. The personalistic norm is one way to express the duty to love, which is so central to Christian ethics based on the Gospel. The use of another person for pleasure becomes the focal point of Wojtyła's treatment of sexual morality, which will unfold in the chapters ahead.

The personalistic norm stands in stark contrast to utilitarian reasoning, which simplistically argues that the right act is always the one that will maximize the state of experience called happiness. Traditional utilitarians identified happiness with pleasure and thereby elevated pleasure to the status of the highest good. Utilitarianism reduces morality to a crude calculation of pleasure and pain, never far removed from the dark shadow of egoism. Wojtyła's critique reveals the many deficiencies of this theory, which is incompatible with the Gospel commandment to love unconditionally.

It should be evident from these pages that sexual love must not be confused with sexual pleasure. It should also be evident that love always requires going beyond oneself to care about the good of the beloved and to affirm the beloved for his or her own sake. Sexual pleasure is only an incidental good that receives its value from the sexual union that expresses committed conjugal love.

# Chapter 4

# What Is the Sexual Drive?

## (Chapter 1: Part Two)

## The sexual drive

The prominent atheist Richard Dawkins has flippantly offered his own version of the Ten Commandments. Instead of "Do not commit adultery," as in the traditional version, he proposes that everyone should simply enjoy his or her own sex life, as long as it doesn't imperil anyone else.[1] Regrettably, the Dawkins version confirms the sentiment of many people who dismiss traditional sexual morality as outdated and old-fashioned. This attitude reflects a convenient misunderstanding that our sexual capacities exist for our own pleasure and amusement. In such a view, sexual activity crosses the boundary of moral acceptability only when it is non-consensual. Wojtyła's extended treatment of the sexual drive demonstrates why these misconceptions are so ill-founded.

Up to this point in his book Wojtyła has considered persons as subjects and objects of action. Sometimes these actions involving two persons are shaped by the sexual attraction between a man and a woman.

---

1. Richard Dawkins, *The God Delusion* (Boston: Houghton Mifflin, 2006), 264.

What are we to call this "dynamic element" between the sexes that can cause much mischief and heartache, but also lead to profound conjugal love? Wojtyła prefers to speak of this sort of dynamism that can activate our sexual powers as the sexual urge or the "sexual drive." He uses this term rather than "instinct," because instinct refers to "a spontaneous way of action" that does not depend on conscious thought (p. 29). But the sexual drive is different. It does not refer to behavior imposed from within but to a natural orientation, a direction in man's life that is latent in his nature.

Man is fully capable of rising above this drive when necessary, but animals are completely determined by the instincts proper to their species. If self-control were not possible for man, it would make no sense to talk about sexual morality and responsibility. Yet sexual morality is a universal phenomenon, something common to all humanity. Every decent society has laws that protect women and children from rape and sexual abuse. And every society recognizes the right to be free from sexual bondage. The sexual drive can create an opening for love and marital intimacy, and so it has an incipient sort of moral value. This is why Wojtyła also refers to this drive as a natural "tending" or aspirational thrust toward another person, which finds expression in action and takes shape under the guidance of reason and will (p. 30).

The sexual drive naturally "happens" in men and in women. It is not an action a person performs, but an event that occurs within a person's body and within his or her emotional life. The person is not responsible for the mere presence of this drive. But he is responsible for what he does in the sexual sphere in response to that drive. If man allows this sexual drive to determine and shape his actions, he relinquishes his precious freedom. Nonetheless, this "happening" creates a foundation for moral action whereby the person takes responsibility for this urge by deciding what specific course of action to pursue. At this threshold, explains Wojtyła, human freedom encounters the sexual drive.

Every person is a "sexual being" shaped to some degree by his or her sexuality, both physically and psychologically. Sexual difference is an original and determining factor of human development, and that difference is obviously more manifest in the body than in the psyche. A person's sexuality "entails a certain orientation" that informs his or her internal, psychological development (p. 31).

At the same time, the different sexual properties of men and women result in an outward orientation or tendency toward the opposite sex. Thanks to the sexual drive, these sexual properties lead to mutual attraction and the possibility of each person being "complemented reciprocally" (p. 32). By contemplating this notion, a man or woman should realize that there is another way of being human that is inaccessible. This revelation exposes the "contingency" or dependency of our existence as sexual creatures (p. 32). It also brings to light the reality that a man or woman needs someone of the opposite sex for the sake of forming a complete whole or unity, especially for the sake of reproduction. Due to the sexual drive, the sexual properties of men and women possess a positive value for someone of the opposite sex, and so we can refer to them as "sexual values" (p. 32). These sexual values are associated with our physical appearance and psychological structure. The sexual drive is the foundation for the value attributed to these sexual properties, including that person's bodily appearance along with his or her masculine or feminine qualities. For example, a woman's physical beauty along with her radiance and femininity are sexual values for a man.

The natural orientation of the sexual drive is always toward a concrete person of the opposite sex, since these properties are always found in a person. It is precisely because the sexual drive is directed toward a particular person of the opposite sex that it can provide a framework for the possibility of love in all its splendor. The sexual drive has the "natural tendency" to develop into conjugal love, the most intimate form of human exchange, since it brings together two persons who share this attraction to each other (p. 33). Thus, sexual difference, which is trivialized in modern society, opens the way for conjugal love whose fullness is achieved in the fruitfulness of new life.[2]

Although conjugal love is born from the sexual drive, it is more than a biological or psychological attraction, because it must be "formed thanks to acts of the will on the level of the person" (p. 33). This sexual drive itself cannot produce action, but it is "the material" that leads to

2. Angelo Cardinal Scola, *The Nuptial Mystery*, trans. M. Borras (Grand Rapids, MI: Eerdmans, 2005), 220–221.

action. Nor does this drive impose itself and deprive man of his inner freedom. No man or woman is at the mercy of the sexual urge the way an animal is at the mercy of its instincts. We like to speak about "falling" in love as if it were just an event that overtakes our whole being. But a married man is not simply overcome by sudden passion and forced into the arms of another woman who is not his wife. Rather, the sexual drive is always under a person's control. He or she must prudently subject that urge to reason, which alone can discern the moral truth about when and how to follow this urge. If the sexual drive is "subordinate" to reason and will, the person can transcend any "determinism of the biological order" through an act of love (p. 33). Nonetheless we cannot forget that the sexual drive is a potent force. We must be prepared to deal with this drive by seeking the prudent middle way: we should neither exaggerate the potency of sexual desire as an irresistible force nor minimize its marvelous potential for enriching marital love.

## The fundamental good of existence

Wojtyła repeatedly insists that this dynamic sexual drive has an "existential meaning," but what exactly does he mean by this phrase? The answer is fairly simple. Wojtyła explains that the sexual drive is not just a biological function at our disposal, to be used however we see fit. It surpasses the biological because "the proper end of the drive . . . is something supra-personal; it is the existence of the species *Homo sapiens*, the constant extension of its existence" (p. 35). The sexual drive at work within the human species ensures the continuing existence of human beings, and existence is "the first and fundamental good" for any creature (p. 35). All other basic human goods derive from this fundamental good of existence.

It is important to bear in mind that existence is not the object of science. Rather, it is the object and focus of philosophy. As a committed Thomist, Wojtyła wants to get beyond the mere concrete *fact of existence* to the underlying *act of existence* by which a being, such as a man or a dog, is really present in the universe. This inner act of presence is the root source of all the perfections within every being. All the perfections a real being has proper to its nature come from its dynamic act of existence, which is naturally ordered to self-communication, that is, to sharing its perfections with others through self-expressive action. At the level of the person, that self-communication becomes self-conscious and free as it begins to assume the form of love, a sharing of one's inner gifts with others. Personhood represents the full flowering of being as an enlightened self-presence (or self-possession). As we have seen, self-possession implies both self-awareness and self-determination. Hence the "proper greatness of this drive," which, through the process of procreation, can bring into being this most intense, personal form of existence, which can enrich the human community by its presence (p. 35).[3]

Although the primary purpose of the sexual drive is procreation, this drive is by no means sub-personal, since it is also the "material" or foundation for conjugal love (p. 36). To some extent, conjugal love must be shaped by the sexual drive with its natural orientation to procreation. Conjugal love can be formed correctly only if it is in harmony with the purpose or "proper finality" of the sexual drive (p. 37). All love is generous and altruistic, caring for and serving the other's good for his or her own sake. When a couple chooses to marry and engage in sexual relations, they have "consciously decided to participate in the whole order of existence" (p. 37). Hence the distinctive feature of conjugal love is that it "serves" the existence of another person, a couple's own child, who is "a confirmation and extension of their own love" (p. 37). A married couple shows their love by welcoming this new person who may come to be through that sexual act. Every couple must undertake the conjugal act with an attitude of love and generosity consistent with the personalistic norm. That love must be extended even to the potential person who has this opportunity to be conceived and to share in the fundamental good of human existence.

Unfortunately, some married people find the purpose of the sexual drive to be a nuisance, and so they try to circumvent it "in an artificial way" (p. 37). But the use of such artificial means often has a corrosive

---

3. See W. Norris Clarke, S.J., *Explorations in Metaphysics* (Notre Dame: University of Notre Dame Press, 1994), 3–12.

effect on marriage. Contraception creates a certain disharmony with nature and interferes with the free gift of one's total self, which is the essence of conjugal love. Authentic conjugal love cannot come to fruition if the procreative capacity of a couple is deliberately stymied, since the contraceptive barrier precludes a full union as one flesh. When a couple deliberately thwarts the procreative process, their love is stripped of its generosity since it no longer "serves" the most fundamental good of existence. Disharmony with nature interferes with the generosity and self-transcendence that are essential for conjugal love to flourish. We cannot justifiably act against nature purely on the personalist grounds that doing so undermines love as reciprocal self-giving.

Too many people, however, falsely see the sexual drive as a biological force with a random purpose that is completely at their disposal. They forget that this drive is not alien to their personhood but an integral part of the unified self that directs them to certain goods. They also fail to appreciate the existential meaning of the sexual drive, which becomes evident only when one takes seriously its true purpose. To regard the sexual drive as a mere biological phenomenon that can be manipulated for any reason deprives that drive of its "objective greatness and meaning" (p. 37). Hence a mature conjugal love always embodies a willingness to procreate, born of generosity and self-sacrifice.

## The religious interpretation

Wojtyła elaborates on the existential significance of the sexual drive in a section of this chapter called "The Religious Interpretation." The sexual drive also directly links persons to the divine order. Whenever a man and woman join together in marriage, they consent to take part in the ongoing work of God's creation, and enter into "the cosmic current . . . of the transmission of existence" (p. 38). Human parents participate in the genesis of a new person, and therefore should see themselves as "rational co-creators" of this new human being (p. 38). They are co-creators because God is directly involved when a new human person is conceived. Why is God's intervention necessary? Wojtyła rejects any materialist philosophy which suggests that the person is merely a physical organism without a soul. Rather, as Saint

Thomas Aquinas has persuasively explained, every person is a natural unity of body and soul. In this life, body and soul are distinct but inseparable—we cannot have one without the other. When a new human being is conceived, the soul must also be created at the same time and united with the new organism. Without the soul infused into the embryo at the time of conception, there would be no development of that being's personal characteristics. This soul, the seat of our intellect and will, must be spiritual since it enables the person to engage in spiritual activities that transcend matter, such as knowledge of abstract ideas. Once we admit the spiritual nature of the soul, it logically follows that this soul cannot be brought into existence except through immediate creation by God. The man and woman involved in the conjugal act are themselves amalgams of body and spirit and cannot create a pure spirit, since the effect (pure spirit or soul) can never be greater than its cause (body and spirit). Thus, the immortal soul, the essence of each person, is the work of God himself. And parents have the great privilege of collaborating with God as his co-creators. A new human person comes into being as the result of love between a man and a woman. But something more than the love of these parents is present at this creation: "the Creator's love decided about a person's coming to be in the womb of the mother" (p. 40).

The sexual drive, therefore, is not a big mystery. Its significance has become distorted thanks to a contemporary sexual ethos that promotes pleasure and self-gratification over love and generosity. But common sense and reason tell us that this drive is associated with the work of procreation, which is part of the natural order of existence under the constant influence of the Creator. When a man and woman enter into conjugal life together, they agree to participate in the special work of creation.

This existential significance of the sexual drive is obscured, however, if our way of thinking is inspired only by the "biological order" of nature, which is an abstraction or creation of the human intellect (p. 40). The study of biology, which has the human body as one of its subjects, "abstracts" or isolates that body as an object of science from the entire body-soul unity that constitutes the human person. The temptation is to allow the biological paradigm to direct our thinking by reducing the person to a material body, or by regarding the person as a kind of machine subject only to the laws of science. When the person is seen in this light merely as the sum of his or her biological functions, the distinctive meaning of personhood is easily concealed. Such a mechanistic conception of man regards the sexual drive purely on the biological plane, a bodily force with no fixed purpose. The temptation toward such abstraction is due to the mentality of empiricism, which assumes that reality is reduced to whatever we can observe through the senses. Empiricism cannot see beyond the surface, and yet it weighs heavily on the modern mind.[4]

Instead, we need to appreciate the sexual drive from the vantage point of the natural order, or what Wojtyła calls "the order of existence" (p. 40). What does he mean by this phrase? Consistent with the natural law tradition, he assumes that there is a cosmic order that reflects God's wise providence. Every real being that exists within the cosmos has its own essence or mode of being that determines what it is. A horse and a cat both exist, but they are designed differently and have different essences. Human beings also have a distinct essence or nature. The human person, like all beings, has a natural ordering toward ends or goods that fulfill his or her nature. Thus, the provident Creator has made the world with a certain created order whereby beings seek fulfillment and enter into interactions or "cosmic relations" in ways proper to their particular design (p. 41). Our human nature includes bodily functions that have a clear and unique purpose: the purpose of the eyes is to see and the purpose of the ears is to hear. Thanks to the soul, a human being is also a person, ordered to basic human goods such as life, knowledge of truth, and marriage, which are connatural to his or her fulfillment. It is vital to underscore that the natural bodily functions and these basic goods are not alien to each other but work together to help the person realize his fulfillment, which has both corporeal and spiritual dimensions. The purpose of the sexual drive, which must always be guided by reason and prudence, is the good of procreation, the continuation of the human species. That drive also directs us

---

4. See Richard Hogan and John LeVoir, *Covenant of Love* (San Francisco: Ignatius Press, 1992), 59–60.

in an anticipatory way to the goods of marital love and family. Those goods foreshadow the final fulfillment of all human beings: total communion with God and with those who have found favor with him.[5]

Wojtyła's point is that we cannot lose sight of this holistic metaphysical vision when we analyze something as important to the person as his sexual drive and sexual capacities. The sexual drive cannot be isolated and abstracted from this order of existence as a mere biological function without its necessary "bond" with the value of existence (p. 41). Rather, one must always appreciate its role within the cosmic order. That role is to further the divine work of creating personal beings who need the nurturing love that can only be provided through the higher goods of marriage and family.

## The rigoristic interpretation

A correct understanding of the existential and religious character of this primordial sexual urge is essential for sexual ethics. Beyond respect for the procreative purpose of sexuality, the relevant issue is how to engage in sexual relations without treating the other person as an object for use or enjoyment. According to Wojtyła, we must avoid two errors. One is the puritanical or "rigorist" interpretation of sexuality, and the other is the "libidinistic" interpretation inspired by Sigmund Freud, who enunciated the "pleasure principle." The former view claims that sex is impure, but it's a necessary evil to ensure the continuation of the human race. Marriage and sexual intercourse are good only when they serve the end of procreation. This view also claims that God himself uses persons as a means to the end of procreation. This rigorist conception of the sexual urge follows the ancient Manichean tradition, which degrades the human body as something evil and alien to the soul. Such

5. W. Norris Clarke, S.J., *The Creative Retrieval of St. Thomas Aquinas* (New York: Fordham University Press, 2009), 90–91. See also J. Budziszewski, "Natural Law as Fact, Theory, and Sign of Contradiction," in *Natural Moral Law in Contemporary Society*, ed. Holger Zabrowski (Washington, D.C.: Catholic University of America Press, 2010), 76–98.

a perception of the body is still embraced by "unilateral spiritualists" who lack the proper balance in their approach to sexual matters (p. 44). Marital intercourse exists not as an expression of love but only as a means to ensure the preservation of the human species.

The rigorists have a deficient notion of anthropology since they see the person as a soul burdened by its body. They also retain a false idea of the relationship between God and his people. God never uses people to bring about any end, however noble it may be. If a man and a woman freely choose to unite in marital union, then that union has moral value and is justified by the true love between them. God has given us a rational nature so that we can freely choose the procreative end of sexual intercourse. And when two people come together to choose a common good such as marriage and family, they should always have a freely given love that manifests itself in sacrifice and cooperation to achieve that common good. To be sure, the Creator wills the preservation of the species, but "preservation based on love that is worthy of persons" (p. 45). In addition, the rigorists fail to see that the sexual enjoyment associated with conjugal sexual intercourse is part of what it means to be an embodied person. In a sound marriage that pleasure is not an end in itself but accompanies the procreative sexual act, which expresses the strong union between man and wife. There is nothing wrong with pleasure of this sort, which serves the good of marriage.

Rigorism seeks to shield a couple from using each other for the sake of pleasure but goes about doing so in a misguided way. The fatal mistake of rigorism is to see even sexual pleasure linked to responsible conjugal intercourse as "a separate end of action," which makes it morally unacceptable (p. 45). It refuses to admit that two people can engage in sexual relations for a procreative and unitive end and enjoy pleasure as a side effect. The joy of harmonious action and sexual union includes the "manifold pleasure" and "the sexual delight that conjugal intercourse brings" (p. 45). However, the rigorist solution cannot escape the trap of utilitarianism. Its prescription of sexual union detached from love purely for the sake of preserving the human species validates the use of persons as an instrumental means for the purpose of bringing about new life.

# The libidinistic interpretation

The libidinistic interpretation, on the other hand, regards the sexual urge in Freudian terms as a drive for the enjoyment that comes from the relief of sexual tension. The sexual urge is conceived as an impulse to enjoy, the consequence of a "particularistic and purely subjectivistic vision of man" (p. 46). According to this viewpoint, this deep-seated desire or urge to enjoy is latent in every human being from his earliest years and needs expression or release. Many of Freud's most ardent followers have argued that liberated personal desire is the key to human contentment. The French psychoanalyst, Jacques Lacan, has even advocated that the principle of acting in conformity with our desires should become the prevailing ethical attitude.[6]

According to this pleasure-centered perspective, procreation is only a secondary or accidental end of sexual intercourse. This idea confuses human psychology with a crude animal psychology, since man is reduced to a subject hypersensitized to pleasure and controlled by his desires. But the libidinistic view fails to come to terms with the "existential" and human character of sexuality. It also neglects to adequately take into account the person's interiority, his reason and will, which precludes abandoning to instinct "the whole responsibility for the [sexual] drive" (p. 47). Thanks to reason, the person can also readily realize that enjoyment is not the sole aim of this urge, which exists for the purpose of procreation. The "libidinistic" interpretation implicitly endorses utilitarianism, because it advocates maximizing pleasure as the supreme moral norm. This hedonistic morality stipulates that sexual pleasure is to be restricted only when it is harmful or non-consensual.

It is instructive to compare the sexual drive with the drive for self-preservation, which is also given considerable prominence in Freud's philosophy. Unlike the instinct to self-preservation, however, the sexual drive is not fundamentally egocentric. Instead, it points us toward

---

6. Jacques Lacan, "The Seminar of Jacques Lacan. Book VII," in *The Ethics of Psychoanalysis*, ed. J.A. Miller, trans. D. Porter. (New York: W. W. Norton, 1992), 314

a life of sharing with others and constitutes the raw material for love. Freudians mistakenly see the sexual drive purely in self-centered terms, but if it follows its natural course, the sexual drive always transcends the limits of the "I," toward a person of the opposite sex. The drive has "as its final end" the gift of existence (p. 50). Because the sexual drive has the opportunity to become generous when directed by reason and virtue, it differs from the instinct to preserve one's self in existence. The libidinistic perspective, which reduces sexuality to a pleasurable experience and overlooks its existential character, remains rampant today and breeds confusion that affects "the whole spiritual situation of man" (p. 50).

# The purposes of marriage

According to both of these interpretations of sexuality, it is perfectly permissible to use another either for reproduction or for pleasure. Both distorted views lose sight of the common good of marriage, which in principle creates the conditions for love rather than use of another person as a mere means to one's own selfish ends. Thus, we can clarify where these interpretations go wrong by reviewing the objective purposes of marriage. It is especially important to appreciate that the natural ends of marriage are incompatible with any subjectivist interpretation of sexuality. Authentic conjugal morality is impossible without this objectivity, without the realization that marriage has a natural end that is willed by God and inscribed in human nature. So what are the ends or purposes of marriage? Wojtyła closely follows the Catholic Church's teaching that there are three purposes of marriage.[7] The primary end of marriage is procreation and the care of children. The second end is "mutual help," whereby a couple forms a unique loving friendship in order to help each other bear the burdens of life. Finally, marriage is a remedy for concupiscence; this end is necessitated by man's fallen state. Wojtyła does not mean to suggest that marriage is a convenient

---

7. See *The Catechism by Decree of the Holy Council of Trent*, ed. J. Donovan (Rome, 1839), vol. 1: 648–650.

outlet for our concupiscent feelings, but that it places one's sexual energies at the service of unselfish spousal love. So marriage thereby overcomes the selfishness that accompanies concupiscence.

These three interdependent ends are achieved through conjugal love as they in turn give that love its direction and proper orientation. In this way, it does not become a selfish or insular love inconsistent with the personalistic norm. The three ends of marriage cannot be properly realized without respect for that norm. Marriage is for procreation, but the conjugal act that leads to procreation belongs to the personal order, and so a man cannot "use" a woman simply to bear his children.

Although marriage has several objective aims, Wojtyła is emphatic about the primacy of procreation, which in "the objective, ontological order" is a more important purpose than that man and woman should live together, complement, and support each other (p. 52). Failure to recognize the fundamental priority of procreation in marriage has created chaos in modern culture, which seeks to redefine marriage as an emotional union that exists purely for the sake of emotional and physical satisfaction. Marriage has a necessary orientation to children that exists even if a couple does not have any children. While the procreative aim has primacy, it is intimately linked with the other two purposes such that they can only be realized in practice as a single "complex fact" (p. 52). Only a sexual act of the generative kind unites spouses in marital friendship in a way that makes proper use of the sexual drive.

Wojtyła's understanding of the sexual drive is central to this theory of sexual morality because it underscores that procreation is the natural purpose of the sexual drive, which is expressed through our sexual capacities and given shape through reason and the will. The use of these powers is usually a pleasurable experience, but pleasure is *not* their purpose. Sometimes the use of our eyes and ears may give us pleasure when we enjoy what we see or what we hear. But the purpose of these senses is not pleasure. The purpose of the eye is to see, the purpose of the ears is to hear, and the distinctive purpose of our sexual drive is procreation.[8]

---

8. J. Budziszewski, *On the Meaning of Sex* (Wilmington: ISI Books, 2012), 21–25.

Since procreation results in children and children need the stability and nurturing of a family, the sexual act should only take place within the context of marriage. As Elizabeth Anscombe explained so tersely, the whole good and intelligible point of the sexual act is marriage.[9]

## SUMMARY

Let us review Wojtyła's argument so far. A wide chasm exists between persons and all other creatures, because only persons are centers of activity with moral independence and an inner life. Hence they deserve to be loved and not used, to be affirmed for their own sake. This is the essence of the personalistic norm, which stands in contrast to utilitarianism that sanctions use of the other for an ulterior motive. A person can also use someone else as an object of pleasure by giving primacy to sexual pleasure, which should only be incidental to the act of sexual intercourse. This second form of use has particular relevance in the area of sexual morality, which focuses on how to preserve justice in sexual relations so they are in harmony with the personalistic norm. The issue of pleasure's proper role cannot be considered apart from the purpose of our sexual powers. In order to understand that purpose, Wojtyła explores the nature of the sexual drive, which is not an instinct but a natural orientation toward another that takes shape through the will and reason. We avoid using other persons in sexual relations only when we keep the existential reality and natural purpose of the sexual drive in view. This means recognizing that conjugal love is for a larger purpose beyond the self: procreation and the bringing into existence of a personal being, which represents the most intense form of existence because of its enlightened self-presence. We cannot act contrary to this purpose by frustrating the natural end of procreation without corrupting the total union of man and woman, which is the essence of marriage. Given its existential significance, sexual relations are suitable

---

9. Mary Geach and Luke Gormally (eds.), *Faith in a Hard Ground: Essays on Religion, Philosophy, and Ethics* by G. E. M. Anscombe (Exeter: Imprint Academics, 2008), 183.

only for marriage, which has three interdependent objectives that are actualized through conjugal love. But what exactly is the nature of conjugal love, and how can we differentiate real love from relationships based on mutual pleasure that only have the appearance of love? Now that he has laid out the necessary ground work, Wojtyła can turn his attention to this central topic.

---

<h3 align="center">Chapter 5</h3>

# The Essential Ingredients of Love

## *(Chapter II: Part One)*

## What is love?

We are morally obliged to love other persons rather than "use" them, but what exactly does "love" mean? There is a good deal of muddled thinking today about the meaning of romantic love, which is often mistaken for an emotional attachment or a purely sexual relationship. Many contemporary writings about the nature and practice of love define it in terms of mutual sexual satisfaction. A recent book about how the French supposedly "invented" love claims that genuine love cannot exist without a radiant sex life. This book reduces romantic love to sexual passion, an irresistible fate to which one must surrender.[1] According to the French—the book argues—in the face of this compelling passion and the forces of amorous eroticism, adultery is sometimes inevitable. So much for fidelity and chastity! Many books like this one glorify sexual desire and pleasure, and some even celebrate hedonistic impulses.

---

1. Pamela Druckerman, "The Annals of Amour," *The Wall Street Journal*, October 20, 2012, C6.

However, they end up conflating romantic love and sexual pleasure, and fail to appreciate the real purpose of sexual union.

It is difficult to sort through the vast literature about love to find a thorough explanation of what love really means. As we noted earlier, few philosophers have addressed this question in a systematic fashion. Like C. S. Lewis, they often distinguish different forms of love such as affection, *eros*, and *agape* (love as charity). Or, like Aristotle and Cicero, they dwell extensively on one particular type of love, such as friendship. Aristotle famously described the friend as "another self."[2] Wojtyła's own account of friendship echoes Cicero's treatise, which defines friendship as "complete sympathy in all matters of importance, plus goodwill and affection."[3] But none of these great thinkers provides the comprehensive definition of love found in *Love and Responsibility*.

Love is a complex reality, complicated by the fact that people mean different things when they use the word "love." Yet Wojtyła bravely sets out to give us an extensive account of love's mysterious character. Love is always a union between persons focused on the good of the beloved. But to understand love fully we must grasp its unitive power as well as its affective and sexual roots.[4]

Wojtyła is primarily concerned with "love between two persons who differ with respect to sex," or what is commonly called romantic love (p. 57). Love is a reciprocal relation between persons based on what is good for each person in the relationship. Love fulfills our longing for goodness in its fullness. In order to explain this broad definition of love, Wojtyła proposes a metaphysical analysis. (By "metaphysical" he means simply a general characterization of love's fundamental elements.) All forms of love possess the same basic qualities, such as fondness and benevolence, and so romantic love is a special manifestation of love in general. This examination of love's common elements opens the way for a psychological analysis that explains how love between a man and

---

2. Aristotle, *Nicomachean Ethics* (Cambridge: Harvard University Press, Loeb Classical Library, 1935), IX, 4.

3. Cicero, *On Old Age and Friendship*, trans. F. Copley (Lansing: University of Michigan Press, 1967), 87.

4. Scola, *Nuptial Mystery*, 55–57.

woman often has its origins deep within the body, senses, and emotional life of these two persons. Love also possesses a personal character or an ethical dimension, since it is a committed and altruistic relationship between two persons. Hence there must be some consideration of love as virtue. In Wojtyła's view, this triadic account of the bond between man and woman—metaphysical, psychological, and ethical—is indispensable for a thorough understanding of love. In this chapter we concentrate our attention on the first stage of this analysis by considering the common traits of love.

# Fondness

Love most often begins as fondness or attraction. One person is initially attracted to another person who is perceived as a good because that person embodies certain values such as a charming personality, a virtuous demeanor, and physical beauty. This attraction amounts to fondness for the other person. In the case of a person of the opposite sex, the attraction is a result of the sexual drive, which must be elevated to the personal level. Thanks to that drive, we are naturally oriented toward the physiological and psychological qualities of a person of the opposite sex. As we have seen in Chapter Four, Wojtyła refers to these qualities as the "sexual values" of a person.

When the fondness is mutual, the barriers between two persons begin to disintegrate as the two are drawn closer together. Fondness for another person engages our reason and will. When a man is attracted to a woman, he commits himself to thinking about her as a good for him, as someone whose presence in his life will enhance his well-being. And since "I want" is always implicit in this sort of fondness, the will also commits itself (p. 59). Thus, the intellect and will help to shape our response to another's naturally good features into the incipient love of fondness. However, emotions play the dominant role, since attraction between a man and woman involves an affective reaction to the sexual and spiritual values of the other person. Emotions are always palpably present at the birth of love because they too help mold "a man's fondness toward a woman and hers in relation to him" (p. 59).

Fondness or attraction is directed toward a specific individual who embodies these sexual values and spiritual qualities, not to the values themselves. A man might be attracted to a woman in part because she has long blond hair, a pretty face, and a sweet disposition. He is conscious of the values that begin to entice him, but fondness is more than the conscious state of awareness of these values. Rather, fondness is directed toward the person who possesses the values, and it proceeds from a person. This is why we can refer to it as love or at least love in its nascent form. Thus, fondness "belongs to the essence of love," though love certainly cannot be reduced to fondness (p. 60).

A person's reactions to another's personal or sexual qualities will depend on his or her sensitivity to particular values, since "someone can be fond of a person in various ways" (p. 61). While one person may be more sensitive and attracted to sexual values, another will be more sensitive and attracted to spiritual and moral values. A young man, for example, is more apt to be moved by sexual values, such as a woman's physical appearance or feminine charm. On the other hand, an older man is more likely to be attracted to a woman who is wise, mature, and caring. Love will evolve and take shape quite differently in these two situations.

The emotions play a critical role in the process of developing fondness for another person. However, this can cause problems because our feelings arise so spontaneously and forcefully that they can overwhelm reason and "hinder fondness of the true good" (p. 61). When that happens, it often leads to an intellectual blindness that impedes one's ability to perceive the full truth about the other. The emotions can falsify fondness when one perceives values in another person that simply do not exist. For example, Peter's growing fondness for Jill leads him to see her as a thoughtful and generous person when in fact this is not the case. Such a situation is dangerous for love because when the emotions subside, they leave one in a vacuum, deprived of the good that one seemed to have discovered.

Even at the level of fondness it is important to recognize and appreciate the truth about the object of one's affections. A person must always be wary of indulging his or her affections at the expense of the truth. Perhaps Peter's fondness and delight for Jill inhibits him from recognizing her weak moral character. Or Mary is wrongly convinced that her self-centered new boyfriend is mature enough for a substantial relationship because she enjoys his company so much. These distortions often result from an inward-looking subjectivism, a self-absorption in emotional satisfaction that is all too common in the early stages of romantic love.

Wojtyła admits that the emotions have a certain truth of their own, but we cannot trust them to convey the whole truth. Any truth suggested by the emotions must be verified and augmented by reason. The truth about the value of the person and that person's objective qualities can be appreciated only on a higher, intellectual level. Both the truth about the whole person as well as the "truth of affections" must coalesce in the proper development of fondness (p. 62). Thus, there must be "two truths" involved in love even at the level of fondness: the subjective emotional truth and the objective truth based on reliable knowledge so that we can appreciate the value of the person along with his or her objective qualities. Both truths, properly integrated, endow fondness with that perfection or proper quality which is necessary for genuine love to evolve.

One must always avoid fixating on one or two of a person's values, such as physical appearance. Instead, one should lovingly respond to the *whole person* along with the goodness of personhood present intrinsically in every individual person. Authentic fondness captures "above all the very value of the person" and appreciates that the focus of attention is "precisely the person and not something else" (p. 63).

The object of our fondness and attraction is always seen as a thing of beauty, and physical beauty often plays a critical role in the attraction between a man and woman. Every woman is beautiful in a way of her own, and she attracts a man's attention by way of her beauty. However, we must not forget that a human being is a person whose personal qualities are determined by his or her "interiority." Therefore, it is necessary to discover a person's "interior beauty" as well as his or her exterior beauty (p. 63). Love might begin as an attraction to a person's visible and sensual beauty, but that attraction must evolve into a deep appreciation for the beauty of the whole person.

# Desire

Desire too is an essential aspect of love. The human person is not self-sufficient and, out of his poverty, reaches out to others to fill his needs. Since every human being is limited by being either a man or a woman, there is an "otherness" and incompleteness within humanity. This creates an interior void so that a man needs a woman to complete his own being, and a woman needs a man in the same way. One sex completes what is lacking in the other sex. A woman's gentleness and compassion balance and temper a man's toughness and pragmatism. This felt need for completeness is manifested through the sexual drive. Relationships between man and woman are not neutral, but depend on this need for the other who will help a person find fulfillment. This accounts for the fact that "love of desire" is different from desire itself, "for it proceeds from a need and aims at finding the missing good" (p. 64).

Desire (particularly sexual desire) presupposes awareness of some lack, but in this case a man desires a woman only as an instrumental means to satisfy his desire. *Love of desire*, on the other hand, represents an objective need for the other person who is good for me and an object of longing. Love of desire is never felt as mere sexual desire but also includes a *"longing for the good for oneself"* (p. 65). Such longing is expressed in the sentiment: "I want you, because you are a good for me" (p. 65). A man longs for a certain woman because he knows that possessing her and sharing his life with her will make him better off and fulfill his deepest aspirations. Union with her will fill the void or lack of wholeness that can only be met by this particular person of the opposite sex. When the poet, shattered by his wife's death, writes that "she was the beat of my heart for many years," we know exactly what he means.

Love of desire should never be equated with sensual desire alone, though sensual desire is an aspect of this form of love. Love of desire presupposes a need that can be met only by another person who is good for me, who will make my life better. Since that good is beneficial, it is also useful, but this does not imply that the person who fills my need is an object of use. A widower seeks a new wife whom he can love and cherish, but who will also be a mother for his young children. She is useful to him in this sense, but if she freely and generously consents to the marriage, she is certainly not being used by him. However, couples must be vigilant that love of desire does not drift into a utilitarian attitude, but is always consonant with the personalistic norm. In the face of love of desire's power and pull, a man and woman should bear in mind two important principles. First, longing or desire for a person of the opposite sex should always include more than sexual desire. If a person merely fills one's sexual needs, there will be no basis for a relationship that goes beyond using that person. Second, they should never suppose that human love "is exhausted completely in love of desire" (p. 66).

## Benevolence

Unlike fondness or love of desire, benevolence directs us farther beyond ourselves to act on behalf of the beloved. Every person finds in true love "the greatest fullness of his being" (p. 66). But what is this true love that has the power to perfect our existence? True love of another person requires actions that support and affirm his or her inner worth and intrinsic goodness. False love, on the other hand, tends to undermine that person's worth and sabotage his or her fulfillment. True love, therefore, must surpass longing and desire for the other. It is not enough to desire union with another person because of that other person's ability to help me achieve my own personal fulfillment. It is also necessary to desire and care about what that other person needs for his or her own flourishing, to perfect himself or herself as a person.

Hence, love must also include benevolence or charity, which will safeguard love of desire from devolving into crude forms of using another. Love as benevolence is captured in Saint Thomas Aquinas' classic definition of love: "To love is to will the good of another."[5] This form of love orients the will in an altruistic way, toward a benevolent caring for the other and an affirmation of the person for his or her own sake. I want what is truly good for this person for her own sake, for her flourishing as a person, not for the purpose of advancing my interests. Thus, in love as charity or benevolence, a person goes beyond longing

---

5. Saint Thomas Aquinas, *Summa Theologiae*, I–II, q. 26, a. 4.

for another person as a good that will bring him some measure of ful-fillment, and instead he also actively seeks the true good of the beloved.

Benevolence is a self-effacing love that overcomes one's natural self-centeredness. It is free of self-interest, and so it must "transcend desire" (p. 66). Love as benevolence is unconditional, selfless love, the highest form of love. Benevolence is love in a more "absolute sense," and it brings us close to the "pure essence" of love; it perfects the person who shares his or her love with another, and brings fulfillment to both lover and beloved (p. 67). Such love or benevolence is essential to a durable relationship between two persons. Married life can be enriched by pas-sionate and sensual desire so long as the spouses also have an abundance of benevolence that is not consumed by that passion. Only where there is benevolence can it be said that there is true love, which makes mutual sharing possible.

# Reciprocity

Since love must consist of mutual sharing, Wojtyła turns to a treat-ment of reciprocity as he continues this review of love's principal elements. Reciprocity is "closely linked with love *'between'* a man and a woman" (p. 68; my emphasis). Love is not something in a man and in a woman, but something common to them both. There is one objective whole, a joining together or union "in which two persons are involved" (p. 68).

The way from one "I" to another is through a commitment of the will, but if this is a one-way street, that love will be one-sided. Love will pos-sess its typical psychological profile, but it will be unrequited. On the other hand, when a man's love is responded to by the same love in a woman, love exists on both sides of their relationship as something *between* them, something mutually shared. Love is bilateral or shared between two persons such that a single "we" arises from two "I's." This reciprocal love produces a whole that is greater than the sum of its parts. Wojtyła explains that "reciprocity is decisive precisely for this 'we' to come into existence" (p. 69). Thus, while love has its beginnings in fondness, longing, and benevolence, it is actually crystallized through the reality of reciprocity. These aspects of love can now be seen in a new light.

In true love, where such reciprocity exists, one person desires another person as a good, and also desires the other person's love in return for his or her own love. Mary may desire Steve as a good for herself because he is ruggedly handsome, honest, tolerant, and a good provider. And since she cares about him, she wants what is good for him (benevolence). But she also wants Steve's love as a response to her love. Therefore, she longs for him as a co-creator of love and not just as an object of desire, because she believes that this will be good for him as well as for her. If Mary's love is requited, if Steve feels the same way and wants Mary's love in return, this couple becomes a "we," who will work together as co-creators in love. Reciprocity synthesizes love of desire and benevolent love, since this community "between" persons transcends self-interest yet fills the needs and desires of both parties. Mary and Steve both *give* and *receive* love and thereby share in the joy of togetherness.

If reciprocity is based on seeking the good of the other along with mutual personal fulfillment, it is profound and mature. But if advantage, utility, or pleasure determines reciprocity, "then it is something shallow and unstable" (p. 69). Authentic reciprocity, based on personal love, brings confidence and reliability to a relationship. These qualities account for the trust that brings about freedom from suspicion and jealousy. Reliance on another person, such as a good friend or a spouse who will not fail in time of need, is the source of great peace and comfort. These "fruits of love" flow forth from love's very essence (p. 70).

On the other hand, if one or both of the persons in this relationship has utilitarian and self-centered aims, there will be no mutual love or caring, but only jealousy and suspicion. One cannot trust a person who is disposed to regard other people only as a means to achieve his preferences. A relationship based on the subjective good of pleasure cannot survive, since the couple will remain together only so long as they bring pleasure to each other. Pleasure and sensual delight are not substantial goods that can unite people for very long. Authentic reciprocity presupposes altruism or benevolence in both persons. It cannot arise from the convenient coincidence of two individuals' self-interest such as the achievement of some sort of mutual satisfaction or preferences. Such arrangements can provide only a semblance of reciprocity.

From this account of reciprocity Wojtyła draws two important conclusions. First, love must be further analyzed from both a psychological and ethical perspective. This analysis can shed light on what it means to develop a reciprocal relationship based on altruism, an absolute concern for the well-being of the other, rather than on egoism, which often lays concealed in our emotional experiences. The more practical conclusion is the need for a couple to test love in order to ensure that there is more than a façade of reciprocity whose only support is their own self-serving interests. Love cannot endure as a combination of "two egoisms," but only as an interpersonal union where a "mature 'we' is manifested" (p. 71).

## Sympathy and friendship

Another key aspect of love needs consideration: sympathy. Sympathy represents affective love, an emotional bond between two people whereby they empathize with each other and experience things together. Sympathy builds on the emotions that accompany fondness by uniting two people. Sympathy creates a "we," but a fragile "we" that depends solely on these coinciding emotions. Rather than an active commitment, sympathy is something that passively "happens" between people. People succumb to sympathy in ways they sometimes find incomprehensible. Thus, sympathy is love at the purely emotional stage where the will barely plays an active role.

In pulling the wills of two people "into the orbit" of emotion and affection, sympathy brings those two individuals closer together and creates an emotional union (p. 72). It awakens a positive affective response toward another person whose company creates an agreeable sensation for me. As a result, I come to prize the person's presence and perhaps I value her more than my other friends. The problem is that sympathy mediates our appreciation of another person's value, and this "implies a hint of subjectivism" (p. 73). For example, Susan has developed a strong emotional bond with Jim because she feels less vulnerable and more "at home" with him. Susan and Jim don't engage in serious conversation and don't even know each other very well, but each one thoroughly enjoys the other's company. Thus, Susan likes and values

Jim, but only because of the way he makes her feel. His frequent compliments and charming manners always seem to lift her spirits. This is a fickle relationship that will probably not survive when the strong emotions recede. Jim is not valued so much for who he is, but for the emotional satisfaction that he brings to Susan's life. As Wojtyła explains, "the value of affection replaces in some sense the value of the person" (p. 73).

Sympathy is not to be dismissed, however, because it has the ability to make people more attuned to each other. A palpable experience of intimacy, sympathy keeps alive a vivid awareness of the other person so that one feels the other's whole personhood. Thanks to sympathy, two lives become closely intertwined: "one lives in the circle of the other, at the same time finding him at every step in one's own" (p. 73). Yet this sympathy or emotional togetherness is by no means the whole of love, as some have supposed, because it is passive and not something actively created by the will.

True togetherness must go well beyond sympathy. It depends on the will and takes shape in friendship, where there is benevolence and charity toward the other. In contrast to sympathy, the direct involvement of the will is decisive for friendship to blossom. In friendship, "I want the good for you as much as I want it for myself, for my own 'I'" (p. 73). The altruism and moral unity of friendship, whereby each person commits himself to the other, is superior to the emotional and tentative unity created only by sympathy. Wojtyła describes that deep moral unity as "a doubling of the 'I,'" where the will relates to both I's "with equal favor" (p. 74). Since the will commits itself, friendship is not something that "happens," but it is a clear and definitive choice of the other person.

The bond of friendship, however, is enhanced by the emotional warmth that sympathy provides. Sympathy must be transformed into friendship, and friendship must be augmented by sympathy. As Wojtyła explains, "In itself sympathy is not yet friendship . . . [because it] still lacks an act of benevolence, without which there can be no true love" (p. 74). But friendship, which is the basis for a sound marriage, is always a moral commitment to another person, which includes truly caring for and rejoicing in the other's good. In Wojtyła's recipe for love we now add the ingredient of friendship, a full mutual commitment that yields a more durable unification of two persons.

Sympathy can mature into friendship only if the person can subordinate his emotional feelings to a sincere concern for the one he loves. Love cannot be merely a matter of sympathy, because love demands a commitment of the will to the good and well-being of the other. But friendship also needs the emotional intensity of sympathy, without which it will be cold and aloof. Without sympathy, two people might still be committed to each other but they do not savor each other's company. On the other hand, a couple's enjoyment of each other, especially as it comes to fruition in a lifelong marriage, is something to be cherished. Hence sympathy and friendship, emotional vitality and mutual commitment, must be carefully woven together in a relationship. They are two processes that must interpenetrate and support each other. Love must have both a subjective and objective dimension. In many relationships sympathy is immediately intense and vivid, while friendship is at first "pale and weak" (p. 75). The mistake many people make is to leave the relationship at the level of sympathy with no conscious and deliberate attempt to transform it into friendship, "this unity of the will thanks to which two 'I's' become one 'we'" (p. 77).

We have now seen that love develops by way of fondness, longing, and benevolence, and finds its full realization in a reciprocal relationship between two persons who become co-creators of love. Love must also include the mutual moral commitment of friendship, which is greatly enhanced by the emotional warmth of sympathy. These aspects of love interpenetrate and are found in all types of love, which always brings the person outside of herself. Love is not just self-transcendence but a "transition from 'I' to 'we'" (p. 78). Love is a "striving" for the other's good and a "uniting of persons," which perfects both the lover and the beloved (p. 78). As we noted earlier, no person achieves self-fulfillment through isolated self-sufficiency but only through love and generosity, which creates interpersonal communion.

## Spousal love

Wojtyła is keenly interested in a particularly profound form of love that can take place between two persons. He describes this personal relationship as spousal love. According to Wojtyła, the essence of spousal love is "giving oneself, giving one's 'I'" (p. 78). All forms of love reach out beyond the self to the other person and seek the other's good, but they do not reach as far as spousal love. The reason, explains Wojtyła, is that to give one's whole self to a person is more than just willing what is good for that person. In spousal love a person gives himself to another person, either to a human person or to God, and through this giving "a particular shape of love . . . is formed" (p. 79). When spousal love creates this "inter-personal connection," it surpasses friendship because there is a "reciprocal self-giving of persons" (p. 79). This is the fullest and most radical form of human love, because it involves handing over oneself to become the possession of another. While other acts of love can involve another person for a short period of time, spousal love *"is linked to the choice of a vocation in the dimension of the whole life"* (p. 285).

Although spousal love can occur between man and God, the most common form is marriage where the love of a man and a woman leads to reciprocal self-giving. Unlike the love of friendship, marriage is a vocation in which two people make a permanent and exclusive commitment to each other that is expressed in a sexual union. Wojtyła will consider marriage more thoroughly in later chapters, but let it suffice to say that this interpersonal union is the fullest possible union of two human persons.

Spousal love is a mystery and a wondrous paradox, so it needs a thorough consideration. How can a person, who is incommunicable, give herself to another? There is no self-giving in the world of nature, where creatures are immersed in matter. But what is impossible in the natural order is quite possible in the world of persons, which is governed by the rule of love. It is precisely because the person consciously possesses herself through self-knowledge and personal freedom that she can give herself *freely* to another. Thanks to a "mature perception of values," the will can commit itself in this radical way (p. 80). A person recognizes the value of giving and chooses to make a gift of himself to another. In accordance with the inner "law of the gift" imprinted on our nature by God, he or she aims for a higher level of generosity than benevolence and friendship. Instead, this person reaches out to love and care for another in the most complete and radical fashion of spousal love. The person decides that his life's vocation is to take shape through a self-oblivious love and devotion to another chosen person.

To be sure, there is something paradoxical about all this. By giving my inalienable self to another I am not diminished in any way. My personhood is not suddenly extinguished or compromised. Rather, reciprocal self-donation allows both individuals to flourish more fully as persons: "this 'I' is not in the least destroyed or devalued, but, on the contrary, is developed and enriched" (p. 80). Thus, I possess myself most completely in the act of self-donation. The experience of opening oneself to this reciprocal self-donation creates a more mature self-possession, a greater self-confidence, and a profound sense of self-worth. As Andrew explains in Wojtyła's drama about marriage, "love tends to broaden and enrich what was narrow and limited."[6]

In giving ourselves, therefore, we find clear evidence that we possess ourselves. Of course, it seems that self-donation comes in many forms. A doctor is dedicated to his patients and a pastor to his parishioners, while a teacher is devoted to his students. However, what might be at work in these cases is simply friendship or benevolence. But even if these forms of devotion were to rise to the level of a fuller self-giving, one could still not apply the term "spousal love." This type of devotion, however commendable, lacks the exclusivity of spousal love, which always entails "the giving of the individual person to another chosen person" (p. 81).

The reciprocal self-giving that is the foundation of marriage is not just something psychological. Spousal love is more than an emotional or psychological experience of giving and possessing. An irregular emotional attachment can sometimes create the appearance of mutual self-donation when only mutual self-interest is at work. For example, Ellen "gives" herself to Walter in marriage because she is weak and immature and needs someone to control her life. Walter dedicates himself to controlling Ellen's life, which he sees as another one of his "possessions." There may be an experience of self-giving in this relationship, a semblance of "giving" and "possessing," but there is no authentic spousal love. Spousal love always entails a wholehearted self-donation and self-surrender, a selfless devotion to the other without ulterior and

---

6. Wojtyła, *The Jeweler's Shop*, Act 1.

egoistic motives. The psychology or experience of self-giving may differ in a man and a woman, but masculine and feminine self-donation merge in marriage and constitute "the mature totality of reciprocal self-giving" (p. 81).

In addition, spousal love should never be confused with self-giving at a purely physical or bodily level. It is especially critical for a couple to avoid the temptation of giving themselves to one another only sexually. This arrangement will undoubtedly lead to relationships based on mutual sexual satisfaction rather than love. Sexual self-giving is justified only by the self-giving of persons. Spousal love is a *total* sharing and *total* union of two persons that is expressed on a bodily level. It always involves other demands that a person has a right to make of the beloved. Thus, if the sexual act is to embody and signify exclusive self-surrender or self-donation, it can only take place within the context of deeply committed conjugal love. It is only by restricting sexual intercourse to one couple that love "can be fully open toward new persons who by nature are fruits of spousal love" (p. 82). Sexual union without a personal union lacks integrity, since the person is saying one thing with his body but quite another with his mind and will.[7]

Although spousal love differs from all other forms of love because of its exclusivity, it cannot develop in isolation from them. It requires benevolence, friendship, and even the emotional warmth of sympathy. Without these trusted allies, spousal love will find itself in a dangerous vacuum, unable to cope with the exigent circumstances that sometimes threaten committed and stable romantic relationships.

## SUMMARY

This whole chapter has explained the chief ingredients of love: fondness, love of desire or longing, benevolence, reciprocity, the emotional togetherness of sympathy, and the deeper moral commitment and unity of friendship. All types of love, therefore, involve a

---

7. See Pruss, *One Body*, 146; 172–73.

self-transcendence and a union of persons. Spousal love is distinguished from other forms of human love because it is characterized by exclusive self-donation that goes beyond willing the good of the other.

Some of these elements, such as benevolence and friendship, are more objective because they are based on the permanent values of personhood, self-sacrifice, and moral commitment. Other elements such as sympathy, which is not always controlled by the will, are more subjective and spontaneous. Love cannot be sustained if it is based merely on subjective elements like sympathy or the superficial fondness that comes from attraction to another's sexual values. These aspects of love are often fleeting and fail to take into account the intrinsic worth of the other person. Love in its subjective profile is really only infatuation, which lacks the sturdy resilience of love based on friendship and benevolence. Real love always rises above the spontaneity and intermittent character of attraction and sympathy.

We now have a much clearer sense of what it means to truly love another person. We can appreciate why real love, which is permeated with an altruistic spirit that affirms the other person for his or her own sake, is so superior to use, even if two people consent to use each other for mutual pleasure. A relationship of mutual sexual satisfaction lacks the selfless generosity and unequivocal commitment that is love's trademark. With this definition of love in mind, Wojtyła now considers how spousal love develops as a psychological attachment that takes root deeply within the body and psyche of a man and a woman.

---

———— ⚜ ———— Chapter 6 ———— ⚜ ————

# The Psychological and Ethical Aspects of Love

## *(Chapter II: Parts Two and Three)*

## Psychological analysis of love

### *Sense impressions and emotions*

Any study of love is incomplete unless it includes some treatment of its psychological dimensions. As we have seen, the components of love include fondness, desire, and sympathy. Wojtyła now considers in more depth the sense impressions and emotions that give birth to these aspects of love. The result of these physical and psychic energies is a psychological state that can falsely appear to be love in its full flowering. If the development of love stops at this point, we end up with truncated forms of love such as affectionate or sensual love. Both the sentimentalist and the hedonist misconstrue the nature of love. But it is also possible that an embryonic relationship energized by sensory and emotional sources will blossom into full conjugal love.

Wojtyła begins this psychological analysis with a brief explanation of our external senses through which objects in the world manifest their presence to us. These senses are a bridge to the outside world, the basic means of contact with other real beings. Each of the five senses has its own distinct mode of receiving data. For example, the ear transmits all incoming data into sounds. The senses, however, should not be identified with bodily organs. The sense of sight is enabled by the eyes and other aspects of the human organism. But that sense imposes its own structure on incoming data and also has a "psychical property" that allows us to "apprehend objects in a certain way" (p. 84).

Wojtyła admits that sense perception is not always completely reliable. Sense knowledge by its nature is somewhat subjective. Nonetheless, through the work of his or her senses, a person is flooded with sense impressions that always contain an image of the object that is "concrete and particular" (p. 85). Our senses react to objects in the outside world based on this sensory impression of the object. How is such an impression formed? Through external sense receptors we receive from an object data that is transmitted to the brain and to the person's consciousness. An impression of the object is constructed from the data, an impression that is relevant to the organism's needs, desires, and lived-experiences. A hungry man will construct a different impression based on the sight and smell of a freshly cooked steak dinner than the man who has just eaten a big meal. These impressions become the basis for how we interpret the world and classify objects with the help of reason. Some impressions are imprinted more permanently and distinctly on our consciousness, while others are feeble and transient. At times, a particular impression will cause a strong sensory reaction or "perceptible movement" in a person's consciousness (p. 85). Hence, the common phrase that a thing or person "made an impression on me."[1]

These sense impressions can also be accompanied by emotions, which are an experience of the values associated with the object perceived by the senses. Our sense data might create the impression of a beautiful sunset, and our emotions react to the aesthetic values of this scene. When emotions are linked with impressions, the perceived object "much more distinctly forces itself into man's consciousness" (p. 86). All

---

1. I have relied on Father Norris Clarke's unpublished "Notes on Epistemology" for this discussion on the senses.

of this has significant implications for the origins of romantic love, where "first impressions" often play a pivotal role. Romantic or spousal love typically begins with such a palpable impression of a person of the opposite sex accompanied by strong emotions. This makes it possible to experience another person as someone valuable or potentially good-for-me, someone worthy of being possessed by me in some way.

## Examination of sensuality

The sensory experience of a person of the opposite sex can easily make a strong impression because of the sexual drive. Emotions will sometimes accompany the impression. This is so because someone of the opposite sex is valuable, that is, good for the person who constructs the impression. When a man sees a woman, his senses convey an exterior image of that woman. The impression constructed is more than just a woman's body, however, but a human being of the opposite sex. The emotions contribute to the "vividness of the impression" (p. 87).

Wojtyła refers to this physical component of love based on sensory image or impression as "sensuality." Sensuality is more than an ordinary reaction of the senses to an object based on an impression of that object. Rather, sensuality is an *experience of sexual values connected with the body of a person of the opposite sex.* Through his senses and the impression they create, Jim has an immediate and emotionally vivid experience of Jane's sexual properties (or values), such as her long blonde hair, her slim figure, and her pretty face. This experience represents sensuality. Sensuality in itself has a "consumer orientation," since it is directed at the body and only glancingly at the other as a person (p. 88). It tends to bypass the person in favor of the body making the strong impression. Sensuality can even interfere with one's appreciation of the body's sexual beauty, because it introduces a utilitarian attitude that regards the body as a potential object for gratification. Sensuality expresses itself as an appetite because it induces us to see someone as an object of desire due to the sexual properties embedded in that person's body.

Although the disposition of sensuality is "spontaneous [and] instinctive" (p. 88), it is not something morally perverse but a purely natural phenomenon. Sensuality differs from a man or woman's sexual vitality, which is developed as the sexual powers grow into maturity. However, there is certainly a connection between sexual vitality and sensuality. The sexual drive, which lies at the root of sensuality, expresses itself through mature sexual powers as it seeks to fulfill its "objective end" of reproduction (p. 89). Sensuality serves that end by drawing a man and a woman into a relationship and perhaps into a sexual union that will achieve this purpose.

The disposition of sensuality is natural, but it does not suffice as a measure of proper behavior in the sexual life. The promptings of sensuality do not provide the necessary moral guidance, since the object of our sensual longing is not just an attractive body but a whole person. And the person demands a different attitude from the one proper to sensuality. Sexual ethics can never be reduced to the emancipation of our sexual desires or a spontaneous following of sensuality, for such behavior will lead to endless transgressions of the personalistic norm.

We know from our previous analysis that a human person cannot be an object for use. We also know that a person is a natural unity of body and soul. As an integral part of the person, the body cannot be treated as if it were an instrument somehow detached from the whole person. Two people cannot pretend they are simply using each other's body for mutual pleasure without using each other as persons, because the person *is* his or her body. The sensual reaction to another person's body tends to devalue the person if it is not brought under the guidance of reason. Any attempt to separate the body from the person in order to control it as an object of use is "contrary to the value of the person" (p. 90).

Sensuality by itself, therefore, is not love and could easily devolve into its opposite: the instrumental using of another for sexual gratification. Although sensuality is oblivious to the moral and spiritual qualities of the other person, it still has a positive function in the evolution of love. As a natural reaction to the sexual values of a person of the opposite sex, sensuality creates an opening toward that person, and thereby constitutes the raw material for true conjugal love. Sensuality, which orients the person beyond himself toward an encounter with another person, could be the point of departure for conjugal love. Love of desire progresses through sensuality, but reason and will must temper and integrate that desire with the "nobler" features of love, such as benevolence and friendship. Sensuality itself is blind to the person, since it is directed only toward the sexual values connected with the body. However, when sensuality is properly integrated through reason, its "characteristic instability" and its tendency to see the other through the lens of a consumer attitude can be overcome (p. 91). A properly ordered sensuality can be a bridge toward self-fulfillment through interpersonal union.

Although he warns about the dangers of unintegrated, spontaneous sensuality, Wojtyła never underestimates the potential of sensual desire to amplify the experience of spousal love. He is not proposing a Puritan ethic or a taming of *eros* that calls for the repression of such desires. Rather, he believes that "sensual excitability . . . can . . . become a factor that conditions even fuller and more ardent love" (p. 91). Wojtyła readily admits the vitality of amorous passion as long as it is always linked with charity and a permanent moral commitment to the beloved.

## *Affectivity and affective love*

Wojtyła's psychological analysis of love also includes a careful treatment of affectivity, which is quite different from sensuality. Direct contact between a man and woman involves an impression often accompanied by emotions, but those emotions need not have sexual values linked with the body as their object. In the case of affectivity, the objects of a person's emotional experiences are sexual values that are not just connected to the body but to the whole person of the opposite sex. A man's masculinity might make a dramatic impression on a woman, and a woman's femininity might make the same sort of impression on a man. For example, a man may be drawn not only to a woman's sensuous appearance, but he may also be impressed by her feminine charm, her glamour, or even her coyness. Enthralled by her feminine qualities and graces, he delights in her company and wants to be with her all the time. This affectivity is the source of affective love, which differs from sensuality because it does not emphasize the body within the sensory impression of the other person. On the contrary, affectivity involves emotions based on sexual values linked to the whole woman or the whole man. Unlike sensuality, therefore, affectivity is not "oriented to consume," and as a result it creates more space for the experience of aesthetic values such as a body's beauty (p. 93).

Affectivity may be free from sensual desire, but it usually involves a longing for intimacy and exclusivity. Affective love, which is closely connected to sympathy, binds people together even if they are physically far apart. It takes over one's memory, imagination, and will by creating a romantic mood that thrives on being close to the beloved even if that closeness is only in one's thoughts and memories. When a man and woman become close in this way, they seek "exterior means of expression for what binds them" (p. 93). Since affectivity does not manifest the same self-centered disposition toward the body associated with sensuality, it is often confused with spiritual love. However, it is far from spiritual love since it is something that happens to us. Moreover, the sudden emotional intimacy of affective love can "shift very easily to the area of sensuality," because sensuality is "hidden and latent in affectivity" (p. 93).

Real love, of course, can never be just sentimental affection because the emotional intensity that drives this relationship cannot be sustained. Such purely sentimental love, particularly when accompanied by sensuality, is what we commonly call infatuation. We see it in the impulsiveness and immaturity of Romeo and Juliet, whose passions spawn a love that lacks spiritual balance and depth. In Shakespeare's play, Friar Lawrence cautions the excited Romeo to love moderately because "violent delights have violent ends."[2] In love's initial stages, emotional feelings can often overpower our apprehension and assessment of another person: "in the field of vision of the person affectively committed to another person, the value of the object of his love expands enormously, usually disproportionately to its true value" (p. 94). Affective love tends to influence our imaginative and cognitive powers so that the sexual and spiritual values of the beloved become idealized.

This sentimental idealization, which is often the fruit of affective love, eventually leads to disappointment. Many people tend to exaggerate the qualities of their beloved, but sometimes exaggeration can be carried to dangerous extremes. For example, since Patty sees her

---

2. William Shakespeare, *Romeo and Juliet*, ed. J. Bryant (New York: New American Library, 1964), Act II, scene 6.

fiancé through the prism of affectivity, she cannot recognize that his penchant for enjoying leisure time and his disdain for hard work are serious vices. In some cases, this sort of idealization can take the form of an idolatrous love. Someone idolizes the beloved and therefore loses himself in her instead of finding himself through her affirmation.[3]

The main flaw in affective love lies in its ambivalence and impotence. It seeks closeness with the beloved but "actually finds itself at a distance from the person" (p. 95). This sort of love is not supported by the objective value of personhood, by the beloved's worth as a person to be affirmed for his or her own sake. Rather, it feeds off subjective and superficial values, such as feminine charm, to which the lover clings. When the other person's deficiencies surface, the emotional intensity— the foundation of the whole relationship—begins to wane and the relationship soon unravels. Women are especially prone to disillusionment when a man's affections turn out to be little more than a pretext for the desire to consume.

Like sensuality, affectivity is plagued by subjectivism because it engenders so much self-absorption. A woman caught up in her own feelings allows them to color the truth about the man she loves and the nature of their relationship. This love is often shallow, based on only a dim understanding of another person's character. Thus, the psychological state of sensual love, affectionate love, or their combination leaves people "separated from each other, although it may seem that they are quite close to each other" (p. 96). These forms of love are far removed from love in its fullness. The altruistic elements of love, such as benevolence and friendship, are conspicuously missing from such tenuous relationships, and their absence creates a distance between people that can never be filled by sensual desire or emotional intimacy. The solution to affective love is not emotional impoverishment. One must build on the emotions to achieve a more substantial relationship marked by maturity, integration, and integrity.

---

3. See Eric Fromm's discussion on this topic in *The Art of Loving* (New York: Harper & Row, 2006), 92.

# The challenge of integrating love

Wojtyła has turned to psychology to better understand the structure of romantic love between a man and a woman. Psychology of a different sort reveals the structure of the human person and points to the soul with its capabilities of reason and free will. The soul makes possible an inner life that revolves around truth and goodness. Free choice of the good and knowledge of truth are closely linked, since freedom is impossible without truth. Man must be able to choose the true good among those many goods that thrust themselves upon him or his freedom will be lost. If he could not view such goods in the light of truth, man would be determined by these goods, which "take possession of him and decide completely about the character of his acts" (p. 97). Thus, when a modest good such as sexual values impinge upon the person and unduly influence his choice, his freedom can easily be compromised.

Romantic or spousal love is born on the foundation of the sexual drive, which endows an individual's sexual properties with a value for someone of the opposite sex. When a person experiences a reaction to the sexual values associated with the body, sensuality dominates. But when a person experiences sexual values associated with the whole person (such as femininity), affectivity dominates, while sensual desire often lurks in the background. Depending upon which of these two psychological energies prevail, there is "affective commitment or passionate desire" (p. 98). These forces are intensely felt and reflect the power of the sexual drive. They tend to become a major focal point of our consciousness and absorb our thoughts and aspirations. But sensuality and affectivity are only love in its "subjective profile," love that is felt by the human subject who has the experience. Such love is unreflective and incomplete, and it "strives for integration both 'in' the person and 'between' persons" (p. 98).

The integration of sensuality and affectivity depends on the exercise of free choice and knowledge of the truth. Every person is gifted with these unique capabilities that allow one to live by the light of reason and love. Love is always an interior matter, a matter of the spirit, because love involves charity or benevolence toward the other along with the moral unification of friendship. This type of personal, selfless love can only be realized through a commitment of the will guided by reason and virtue. Love also requires freedom because "what does not carry marks of free commitment, but has the mark of determination and coercion, cannot be acknowledged as love" (p. 99). A woman cannot freely enter a loving relationship if she is driven into the arms of her lover by intense emotions and libidinous forces that blind her to the man's true qualities. She has put herself at the mercy of these forces and therefore lacks the capability to make a sound and free personal commitment. Authentic love demands a fully mature commitment of the will. This commitment must be based on the objective truth of the other person, which goes beyond the pressure of subjective feelings. Love's foundation can never be the shifting sands of subjective truth derived from affectivity or sensuality and based on distinct sensations with an "appetitive tint" (p. 99). Emotionally charged sensory reactions are ephemeral; they are not focused on the whole person but on his or her sexual values. Real love, instead, originates only in a free commitment of the will made in the light of objective truth.

# Ethical analysis of love

## *The value of the person*

It follows from our analysis that psychological situations arising from the experience of sensuality and affectivity cannot supply the appropriate ethical norms for romantic relationships. If this were the case, our subjective experiences and feelings would have primacy over virtue and even love itself. The philosophy of situationalism or "situation ethics" not only repudiates fixed moral principles but also fosters a false view of freedom, which is regarded as emancipation from universal moral duties so that one can do as one pleases. Such simplistic views of freedom fail to recognize that genuine freedom requires the discipline of morality.

Wojtyła has already posited and defended the personalistic norm, which calls for the affirmation of each person for his or her own sake, as a rebuttal to situationalism. The personalistic norm grounds all interactions between persons and represents altruistic love in its most rudimentary form. But a deeper ethical analysis is essential for two reasons. First, as we have observed, love in its fullness includes the virtue of charity or benevolence. The psychological experience of love "must be subordinated to love as virtue" (p. 103). Second, love also includes the moral commitment associated with friendship or the deeper spousal love that gives birth to reciprocal self-giving. Authentic commitment and self-donation must be free, and freedom is conditioned on knowledge of the truth about the good.

The particular focus of this ethical analysis of love is how spousal love can be freely embraced and realized as a virtue. Without the presence of virtue, "there can be no fullness of the lived-experience of love" (p. 103). In the midst of affective commitment and passionate desire, spousal love must never lose sight of the person. Accordingly, Wojtyła lays out four ethical requirements of spousal love, beginning with the need to always affirm the value of the person.

## Affirmation and commitment

Since affirmation is based on the incomparable value of the person, Wojtyła reasserts some of the key assumptions he introduced in the book's opening pages. The person possesses "spiritual perfection," because only a person has an interior spiritual life (p. 104). This person is an embodied spirit, not merely a living physical body. Thanks to the soul, which shares its spiritual life with a body, the person is endowed with the powers of intellect and will. It is fashionable today to speak loosely about the so-called creativity and intelligence of animals, but an "impassable abyss" exists between the psyche of an animal and the spirituality of the human person (p. 104).

Every person possesses value first and foremost as a person. The sexual values, therefore, have only a secondary importance. The value of personhood is linked with a person's whole being and not just with his or her sexual properties. From a psychological perspective, however, love is usually experienced in its earliest stages as a reaction to sexual values attached to those properties. On the other hand, the more spiritual value of "personhood" does not make the same immediate and vivid impression because the senses cannot perceive it. As Wojtyła explains, "the person as such is not the content of an impression" (p. 105). We cannot construct an image of person or soul—it can only be grasped by the mind and known by its lived presence as a source of spiritual activity. This means that the reaction to the person will not be as direct or immediate as the reaction to the sexual values linked with that person's body. An excited young man may easily forget that the beautiful, nicely dressed woman standing before him is not just an object for his enjoyment but a person. She is far more than an attractive body but a *someone* with a soul and her own inner life.

Thus, we must look at each person of the opposite sex in a way that integrates or keeps together his or her personhood and sexuality. Love demands integration, which means the subordination of sexual values to the value of the person. Love must be an affirmation of the person for his or her own sake, or it is not love at all. When love is not permeated with that affirmation, it is at best a "disintegrated love," despite its romantic overtones (p. 105). All this means that while a woman's sexual values and other qualities may play some role in a man's love for her, the sufficient and paramount reason for loving her is to be found in the fact that *she is a person*.

When relationships deepen and two people become bound more tightly together, affirmation grows into commitment. The essence of love is the virtue of charity or benevolence, which always seeks to commit itself or bind itself to another. And since valid commitment requires freedom, which depends on truth, love is always the authentic commitment of one person's free will based on the truth about another person. Love as virtue is a matter of a person's will, which commits that person to another based principally on the value of personhood and that ultimately justifies our loving the person. This positive disposition toward the value of the person is the source of affirming the person for his or her own sake. Affirmation should come to permeate "all reactions, lived-experiences, and all conduct in general" (p. 106).

There is no need, however, to completely suppress sensuality and affectivity, the source of fondness, desire, and sympathy. Rather, these experiences must be integrated with the value of personhood so that they never overwhelm the will's fidelity to that value. This is vital, explains Wojtyła, since "love turns neither to the 'body' alone nor even to the 'human being of the other sex' himself, but precisely to the person" (p. 106).

It stands to reason, therefore, that love cannot be based on sensuality or affectivity alone. Such forces do not permit or lead to this affirmation that is so necessary for love's proper development. Above all, they prevent us from seeing the other *as a person* with all that this implies: an individual with her own deep interior life, capable of acting freely and independently, made for fulfillment and for communion with others. The person should not be treated as an object of pleasurable use even if he or she consents. This is why Wojtyła says that although emotional love brings people closer together, it can easily "deviate from the 'person'" (p. 107). Unintegrated affectivity usually does not lead to affirmation of the person, because the person who experiences this form of affectivity is too self-absorbed to recognize the other's good. Such love is also capricious and lacks the "mature interior cohesion of the kind demanded by the full truth about the person, who is the proper object of love" (p. 107).

Nonetheless, this affirmation of the other for his or her own sake must prevail over the erotic and emotional experiences based on sensuality and affectivity. Such affirmation can proceed in one of two directions. A person in the grip of an erotic experience must either exercise self-mastery and chastity or seek to pursue the vocation of marriage if the affection seems to be mutual. If a person chooses marriage as her life's vocation, she chooses this man, who is the object of her erotic experience, as the companion of her life and thereby affirms him as a person.

## Belonging exclusively to another

As we have seen, marital or spousal love commits the person to self-giving in a profound way. Authentic self-donation must take place on the level of the will, in the free gift of one's whole self to another so that the two persons belong to each other. This type of love leads a person "to stop being his own exclusive possession and to become the possession of the other" (p. 108). The giving of oneself in this radical way does not lead to personal impoverishment but to the self's expansion and enrichment. It is the nature of any being to communicate or give itself, and at the personal level such self-manifestation is conscious and free and thereby turns into love in some form. The drive to share one's goodness or inner riches is called the "law of the gift" or the "law of 'ecstasy'" (p. 108). For human persons, this law, imprinted on our nature by the Creator, is most completely and clearly realized in spousal love.

Reciprocal self-giving creates a "reciprocal belonging" whose expression is sexual intercourse. Sexual surrender is meant to be a ratification and expression of this mutual self-giving or else it becomes mutual sexual gratification. According to Wojtyła, the union of two embodied persons "must be achieved by love, and then sexual intercourse between them can be an expression of this mature union" (p. 109). Sexual relations without interpersonal union cannot be an expression of conjugal love. In these situations, there is a lack of integrity and a disharmony, since the person's body is not integrated with his or her mind and will.

It is morally necessary, therefore, to maintain this sequence or priority, in order to ensure that sexual relations represent an expression of a mature interpersonal union. There must first be a union of persons achieved by selfless love, and "then sexual intercourse between them can be an expression of this mature union" (p. 109). This requirement goes along with Wojtyła's insistence on the primacy of the objective profile of love. The subjective dimension of love is a psychological state based on the experience of sexual values, which occur within a human subject or within two human subjects who are stirred by each other's sexual values. But the objective dimension of love involves charity, friendship, and interpersonal union, and it is decisive. Love always aims at unifying two people through reciprocal self-giving. Sensuality and affectivity can only create the conditions "among which this fact becomes reality" (p. 110).

The "natural greatness" of spousal love derives from "the interior need to give one's person to another person" (p. 110). The measure of this greatness is the supreme value of this personal self that is given to another. Spousal love is reciprocal, a mutual giving and receiving that requires a certain skill. Proficiency of giving and receiving must be developed in light of the value of personhood. A person can give herself only if she is acutely aware of the value of that personal self that she puts into the hands of another. At the same time, she must be conscious of the value of the personal self that is given to her in return. The gift of self is the greatest of all gifts, and it should awaken our gratitude and inspire awe when it occurs. But this gift is surely trivialized if it happens only on the sexual level. Sexual union without an interpersonal union deprives love of its depth and grandeur of self-giving. Thus, it is only in light of the value of the person and power of personal commitment that the "objective greatness of spousal love, of reciprocal self-giving . . . becomes understandable and transparent" (pp. 111–112).

This second ethical requirement of spousal love, which demands that interpersonal belonging and union always takes priority over sexual union, is essential to conserve the authenticity and "greatness" of spousal love.

## *Choice and responsibility*

The third requirement is the need for a mature responsibility in choosing and caring for a spouse. Spousal love is a binding choice to give oneself fully to the other. With that choice comes a special responsibility: not only for the beloved, but also for my own love. Is my love mature and stable enough to justify the other's trust along with the hope generated from this love? A lover has the responsibility to ensure that the beloved will not lose her soul in a relationship but find the "greater fullness" of her existence (p. 112). In a relationship based primarily or exclusively on the experience of sexual values, the reality and true relish of love eludes both partners, and so does any sense of responsibility or altruistic concern for the true good and fulfillment of the other person. But love divorced from responsibility for the other person is a negation of itself, merely a form of egoism in disguise. When a person loves someone, she goes beyond herself and cares more about the true good and welfare of the other than her own well-being. As Aquinas puts it, "A person is placed outside himself when he does not care for the things which are his own, but comes to care for the good of others, and this is charity."[4]

---

4. Saint Thomas Aquinas, *Super Epistolas Sancti Pauli Lectura*, ed. P. Raphaelis (Turin: Marietti, 1953), II Cor., c. 12, lect. 1. See also McAleer, *Ecstatic Morality and Sexual Politics*, 70–71.

If the beloved is to find the fullness of her existence in her spouse, there must be some assurance that the relationship will lead to "some expansion of one's 'I,'" through the possibility of mutual sharing (p. 112). The capability of finding oneself in another is impossible with creatures, immersed in matter, that are always "impenetrable" to each other (p. 113). But persons are not self-contained. Rather, they are spiritual, self-possessing beings. Only a person can freely open himself to another person, and through this interaction and the other's mediation come to better discover himself.

This discussion suggests the challenge of properly choosing a husband or wife. Such a choice is a delicate matter because one is not only choosing a person but another "I," or "oneself in the other" (p. 113). The choice must always have a personal character. Both lovers must keep in mind that they are being entrusted with another person's well-being and fulfillment. A man must be able to find himself in his wife, and she must be able to find herself in him. Spousal love achieves the interpenetration of two lives which "live in and by each other" (p. 113). Such love is impossible, however, for two individuals who are so incompatible that they will inevitably lead disconnected lives and become alienated strangers to each other. A man and woman must make sure that they are suitable for each other so that they can truly belong to each other.

The choice of a husband or wife will depend to some extent on sexual values, if love is to have sexual overtones. Sexual values cannot be discounted if sexuality is to be the basis for "the whole interaction between persons of different sex" (p. 114). But those values obviously cannot be the sole motive for the choice of one's mate. If physical appearance becomes the only reason for the choice of a spouse, that choice will inevitably lead to an unstable marriage. The problem with choice based on spontaneous sexual values is that, despite their intensity, they are undependable and intermittent. Sensual and emotional values ebb and flow, and ultimately diminish over time. Hence, if love is based on the coordination of sensual and emotional experience, it will not endure. The primary motive in choosing another is the value of the person. One must bear in mind that one chooses a person and not the values linked to a person. In true love "a man chooses a woman and a woman [chooses] a man not merely as a 'partner' for sexual life, but as a person to whom he or she wants to give his or her life" (p. 115). When the allure of sexual values subsides, the value of the person still remains and the "interior truth" of love becomes apparent (p. 116).

Moreover, real objective love is always founded on the truth about the *whole person*, whom I choose to love and care for. Wojtyła exhorts his readers to choose and to love the *real* person complete with "his virtues and vices, in a sense independently of the virtues and despite the vices" (p. 116). We cannot love the person as we imagine or wish him to be. The strength of love based on choosing the real person, with all his worthy and unworthy attributes, becomes evident when the beloved person succumbs to weakness or sin. In this case, the one who loves will not withdraw that love in the face of his or her spouse's vulnerability. "Affection, which follows the value of the person, is faithful to man" (p. 117).

It is helpful to think about an example that illustrates this important teaching about the choice of a prospective spouse. When Patty chooses Sam as a husband who will be good for her, she must always remember that he is above all a person. He is a *somebody* with his own interior life and spiritual resources, who is seeking to discover and fulfill himself with the help of others. He is not just a virile, handsome man with an engaging personality who enjoys her company and gives her pleasure. If she decides to marry Sam, she takes on some responsibility for helping him achieve this fulfillment. She must also choose him based on his virtuous habits as well as his character flaws. Patty must face up to his shortcomings, such as his authoritarian tendencies and his occasional jealousy. She must not see him through the deceptions of pride nor let her choice be obscured by sexual values like physical appearance or manly vigor. In a mysterious way, she chooses to give herself to this whole, complex human person primarily because he is a person to be loved. Of course, her choice is also motivated to some extent by his sexual values and his character; she chooses Sam because of his strengths and virtues and despite his persistent vices.

## Love and freedom

What distinguishes the person from the rest of creation is freedom. Freedom exists for love, to deliver us from the bondage of selfishness. Freedom not placed in love's service is "something negative," and gives us a sense of emptiness (p. 117). At the same time, spousal love demands freedom. If reciprocal self-giving is to be authentic, a person must give himself or herself freely. Otherwise that self-giving is deprived of its high quality and its ability to perfect each person in the relationship. In Wojtyła's view, only true knowledge of the other person makes possible a free commitment to him or her, which opens the way for spousal love. Authentic commitment is possible only when it is based on the truth about another person rather than a distorted image shaped by sub-rational emotions. Any commitment, no matter how resolute, based on the coercive influence of sensual desire or extreme sentimentality is not free.

As Wojtyła explained in some depth in his book *The Acting Person*, while our will always seeks what is good, it cannot allow any particular good, such as marriage, to be imposed upon it, or there is no freedom. Sexual values have a tendency to impose themselves and impede freedom, whereas the value of the person "awaits affirmation and choice" (p. 117). A conflict often arises between the sexual drive and freedom when sexual values take possession of man's experience, attempt to overpower the will, and "create in man an interior *fait accompli*" (p. 118). When sexual values beset the will in this way, there is no freedom. The person loves freely only when he commits himself to "another human being as the person whose value he fully acknowledges and affirms" (p. 118). Mary chooses Frank freely only when she recognizes and affirms that he is not a bundle of sexual values but a unique person with his own personal needs, hopes, and aspirations. On the other hand, if the will blindly submits to affectivity and sensuality, it cannot make a creative contribution to love.

What is that grand contribution made by the will? Through the will's creative power a person is capable of transcending herself to care for and celebrate another person's good. The longing and desire for union with a person as a way of achieving fulfillment is secondary to a longing for the absolute good of that person, "the good 'without limits'" (p. 119). I need this person's love for my own well-being, but more than that, I seek and celebrate her fulfillment and happiness.

The will, working in collaboration with reason, has the power to integrate and govern the sexual drive so that it assumes a generous rather than a selfish character. The sexual drive left to its own devices wants "to make use of the other person," but love wants "to give, to create the good, to make happy" (p. 119). The more the sexual drive allows itself to be guided by reason and will operating in the light of truth, the more generous it becomes. The attitude of charity fashioned by the will opens the body and its libido to the other so that the body is no longer a vehicle for sexual transgression, but a means for the exclusive gift of self that we call spousal love.[5]

If a person wants what is truly good for another person, "the good 'without limits,'" he wants God for that person, since "God alone is the objective fullness of the good" (p. 120). Union with God is our final goal, because only God's infinite goodness can fulfill us. Yet only persons of deep faith can recognize this truth.

The moral power of love lies precisely in this sincere longing for the other person's true good. And since a person is capable of such self-transcending altruism, the belief in his or her own spiritual powers is reinforced. By affirming the value of the other person for his or her own sake, I reaffirm myself. I recognize that I am capable of going beyond myself to care about another person and to receive that person's love and care in return. When this sort of selfless love is brought to fruition, it is an "encounter with what is absolute and ultimate" (p. 121). Perhaps Wojtyła has in mind that when people love in this way they more closely imitate their Divine Trinitarian Source through the shared goodness involved in giving and receiving love.

## SUMMARY

In this intricate section of *Love and Responsibility* Wojtyła has explained the psychological state of love, which accounts for certain aspects of love such as fondness and sympathy. Romantic or spousal love receives some of its energy from sensuality and affectivity. Sensuality refers to the emotional experience of sexual values bound up with the body, while affectivity is the experience of sexual values that pertain to

---

5. McAleer, *Ecstatic Morality and Sexual Politics*, 52–53.

the whole person. Sensuality and amorous sentimentality, however, are never adequate to sustain love in a relationship over the long term. Affectivity can cause some attunement between two persons, but the essence of spousal love is interpersonal self-giving and receiving. This reality can only be achieved if sensuality and affectivity are integrated with the higher aspects of love such as benevolence and friendship. The need for integration leads Wojtyła into a prolonged discussion of love's ethical dimension. Specifically, how can spousal love be realized or lived out as virtuous love?

In response to this question, Wojtyła proposes four ethical requirements. First, spousal love must always include an affirmation of the value of the person along with a sincere commitment based on that unconditional affirmation. Second, priority must be given to interpersonal union over sexual union or emotional attachment, the objective contours of love over its subjective contours. Third, spousal love always entails the attitude of *responsibility* for the other's well-being and ultimate fulfillment. In spousal love two lives become interwoven, and this implies the need to choose prudently so that the beloved can find herself in her spouse and he can find himself in her. Fourth, spousal love requires freedom, since the act of self-donation can only be authentic if a person freely gives himself to his spouse. A person cannot choose freely if sexual values beset the will, but only when a commitment is made to a person that affirms and acknowledges his value as a person. In freedom the will can be generous, and love's generosity extends from spirit to body, which now participates in this desire to give rather than take. Wojtyła's ethical analysis of love brings to light why personal fulfillment does not lie in sexual satisfaction, but in an intimate relationship that entails mutual affirmation, commitment, and belonging.

---

Chapter 7

# Interlude

Before we move forward it would be good to review our progress. In his investigation into the various aspects of love, Wojtyła has also shown that love takes different forms. He does not consider all forms of love, such as love of God or parental love, because they are not the focal point of his analysis. His goal is to consider spousal love, but to do this he examines the more common modes of love, especially friendship, which are incorporated into spousal love.

The most basic form of love is benevolence or kindness to others. This love is expressed in the personalistic norm that requires everyone to affirm the value of the person in every situation. Deeper forms of love, like reciprocal self-donation, evolve from this basic attitude of respect for the reasonable ends and legitimate yearnings of other persons. We must transcend our own limits and self-interests in order to give a person enough room to act for himself and to be himself. On the other hand, any instrumental use of a person, whether he or she is a stranger, a friend, a relative, or certainly a spouse, is an abuse of that person's selfhood. Every person deserves benevolence and respect that affirms his or her personal dignity. We might refer to this type of love as "fraternal love," expressed in the commandment to love one's neighbor as oneself.

The second level of love is friendship, which can have varying degrees of intensity. What is common to all forms of friendship is a mutual commitment of the will to one another's good. Mutual affirmation and shared goodness leads to the unification of these two persons. Added to benevolence and kindness is the "clear choice" of another person as the object of care and affection (p. 74). Friendship is more than a psychological attachment or an emotional bond, but the emotions can enrich and energize a friendship.

Like friendship, spousal love is an interpersonal union, but of a quite different kind. Spousal love includes an affirmation of the other person for his or her own sake, which creates an opening for a deeper altruistic love. It also includes the moral commitment of friendship, but in this case the commitment is permanent and unconditional. Fraternal love is *universal*, the love of friendship is *selective*, but spousal love is *exclusive*. Spousal love in its marital form is mutual self-donation that is expressed in the one-flesh sexual union of a married couple. In spousal love, a husband and wife are permanently and exclusively bound to each other. Because of its exclusivity and total self-surrender, spousal love differs from all other forms of love, including maternal or paternal love. A man does not "surrender" himself to his son the way he does to his wife.

In any of these three forms of love, including friendship and fraternal love where the opposite sex is involved, the sexual values experienced as sensuality and affectivity can interfere with love's proper development. Love is fundamentally the virtue of benevolence or charity, a promise to care for the other's well-being. It is not a sentimental feeling or a bodily passion. Like all virtues, therefore, love requires judgment and a commitment of the will. Love as promise and commitment also requires freedom, and freedom depends on truth. The sexual values, however, tend to be intrusive as they thrust themselves upon us, whereas the value of the person must be actively chosen and affirmed. If the passions aroused by sexual values cloud the intellect's good judgment, then the will becomes their servant and freedom is impossible. This situation can lead to violations of the personalistic norm, where one simply "bypasses" the person for the sake of sexual gratification. A woman easily becomes the object of masculine *eros* when she is not loved and affirmed for her own sake. Uncontrolled passion can also lead to an inauthentic commitment or a defective spousal relationship grounded only in subjective reality. Love requires freedom based on truth, seeing the beloved not through the lens of sexual desire or sentimental idealization but for who she really is. For only true knowledge of a person makes it possible to commit one's freedom to her.

However, Wojtyła does not suggest that sexual desire be repressed or that the sexual values be neglected. Rather, it is necessary to tether those values to the value of the person, the most intense expression of being as active presence. Sexual values must be properly integrated so as to always give priority to the other person's well-being and happiness. He or she must not be deprived of the loving-kindness and concern needed for fulfillment and mature self-possession. According to Wojtyła, "the great moral power of true love lies precisely in this longing for the happiness of the other person, that is, for his true good" (p. 120). Sexual values can certainly invigorate spousal love, but they must always be assigned their proper place. They must be subordinated to the value of the other as person and to his good and fulfillment.

Freedom, truth, and love are closely interrelated. If the will is not free because it simply defers to sensual attraction and emotional attachment, there can be no love. But when sensuality and affectivity, love in its subjective profile, are properly integrated, the intellect can recognize the other as a person deserving respect, and it can also appreciate the objective truth about that person in her entirety. Once this truth is fully acknowledged, the will's "creative power" can be engaged by guiding a person's desire to do what is good for his or her beloved, by delighting in that good, and by accepting the other person's love in return. Charity and friendship are always the central players in love's drama, but their performance is enhanced by a "supporting cast" that includes fondness, longing, and sympathy.

We must love everyone because they are persons, but we do not love everyone in the same fashion. All love results in a union between two persons, but spousal love is an interpersonal union of total sharing and total commitment at a bodily level. It is easy for some to confuse a passionate sexual union with an authentic personal union. But when the "nobler elements" of love, such as benevolence and sincere friendship, are missing, there is no complete moral unity of these two individuals *as persons* (p. 90). In this case, the two persons involved have only a sexual or bodily union without a sharing of their two lives that fully embraces them. This results in an alienation or disharmony between the person and his or her body, which becomes a means to dishonestly use another rather than to express love. Both persons are deprived of the dignity of giving, "expressed by [the] body through femininity and masculinity," which leads to mutual full communion and self-fulfillment.[1] Since our sexuality can easily interfere with our ability to form such an authentic personal union of total sharing, a compelling need emerges for the virtue of chastity. Without chastity, the beloved's good as a sexual being cannot be willed in a proper way. We turn to the important theme of chastity in the next chapter.[2]

---

1. John Paul II, *Man and Woman He Created Them: A Theology of the Body*, 259.
2. Pruss, *One Body*. See the first chapter, "Love and Its Forms," 8–48.

# Chapter 8

# Chastity

## *(Chapter III)*

The institution of marriage is under siege, perhaps as it never has been before. Besides concerted efforts to redefine marriage, infidelity appears to be rising. One alarming trend is an increase in infidelity among women. Recent studies suggest a disappearance of the infidelity "gender gap," with 23 percent of married men and 19 percent of married women admitting to extramarital affairs.[1] Some of the reasons for this trend echo Wojtyła's worries about the dangers of individualism with its inward focus on one's self-fulfillment. Some women feel that they are not "fulfilled" in their marriage, and they seek the more extreme emotional attachment that comes with a new relationship. The media are also partly at fault for helping to fray the bonds of marriage. Television shows and movies commonly deal with extramarital sex and adultery, and often portray women as the instigators and seducers. The depiction of lust and loose sexual behavior among married couples fosters a complacency about adultery, even a sense that it's no longer a taboo.

---

1. Peggy Drexler, "The New Face of Infidelity," *The Wall Street Journal*, October 20, 2012, C3.

# Resentment of chastity

To withstand the temptations of lust or sexual indulgence the virtue of chastity is required as a means of supporting the virtue of love. But chastity needs to be rehabilitated and once again welcomed in the human soul. Chastity's "good name" and tarnished reputation must be restored because it is often misunderstood and belittled in secular culture. The motivation for maligning chastity often springs from resentment, which tends to demean high moral standards precisely because they are difficult to achieve. It is far easier to follow conventional morality, dominated by utilitarian premises that exalt pleasure as a superior moral principle. According to Wojtyła, resentment devalues the virtues and true goods that offer us authentic flourishing. With the image of the true good falsified, a person is easily dissuaded from aspiring to that good. Instead, she takes the easier path and recognizes as good only what is convenient, what suits her arbitrary desires. A woman might conclude, for example, that lifelong marriage is an impossible ideal and so she opts for casual sex instead. As a result, chastity "has been deprived by resentment of many rights in the human soul, in the will and the heart of man" (p. 126).

In the wake of the sexual revolution, any advocacy of chastity is often characterized as a fear-based and irrational reaction to the problem of sexually active adolescents. Some Freudians still argue that chastity is harmful to mental health since it involves the repression of the sexual urge, which needs expression. The proposition that "a young man must have sexual relief from the tensions caused by the sexual urge" seems almost a given in modern society. Chastity has many prominent adversaries. These include the German philosopher Friedrich Nietzsche, who viewed asceticism or a chaste lifestyle as a futile effort to repress the sexual demands of the body. The virtuous try to abstain, writes Nietzsche, but the "hound of sensuality looks with envy at everything they do."[2] Still others are not ashamed to openly endorse hedonism as a person's only reasonable and worthwhile goal. Thus,

---

2. Friedrich Nietzsche, *Also Sprach Zarathustra* (Stuttgart: Philip Reclam, 1959), 48.

chastity is seen as a hindrance to erotic love, a foolish alternative to the option for uninhibited sexual enjoyment, which becomes more easily realized thanks to contraception and reproductive technologies. Yet without chastity's discipline, sexual relations can never become anything more than mutual sexual satisfaction.

As a consequence of this prejudice, the practice of chastity is no longer the norm for those who are not married. At the same time, chastity is often misconstrued as sexual restraint purely for its own sake. But, as Wojtyła teaches, this virtue entails much more than sexual restraint. Chastity is a disposition that enables us to perceive the dignity and worth of the other person, and to elevate to the personal level our reactions to sexual values. Chastity is a necessary condition for love. With the aid of chastity the one-flesh union of the conjugal act becomes a true, inter*personal* union.

Many people are confused about chastity because they tend to associate love with infatuation, with the romantic intimacy generated so suddenly by sensuality and emotional sentiment. However, those intense but short-lived experiences cannot constitute the foundation of a durable relationship. The psychotherapist Rollo May described the case of a woman we'll call Sharon. She came from a stable, upper-middle-class family. Sharon married soon after college as she was expected to do and quickly had five children. But out of loneliness and apathy for her husband, she fell in love with her garage mechanic. Her therapist tried to get at the bottom of all this and steer her back to her husband, but Sharon would have none of it. The relationship, fueled by passion and drama, was "too sacred," she said. Sharon was convinced that she was deeply in love, but within months the relationship crumbled and she was left alone to care for her children. Whatever issues she and her husband may have had, Sharon clearly took a desperately wrong turn in her life. She fell into a tentative relationship based only on torrid passions that could not possibly be sustained. She then had to confront the emptiness that inevitably results whenever one substitutes passion and emotional exuberance for romantic stability based on commitment and mutual affirmation.[3]

---

3. Rollo May, *Love and Will* (New York: Dell Publishing, 1969), 118–119.

As we have seen, true conjugal love must include charity and friendship that are ratified through sexual intimacy. Sharon and the mechanic had no moral commitment to each other, no real caring for one another. The shallow bonds between them were based purely on precarious emotions and sensual desire. Hence there was no love, but only a thrilling amorous experience masquerading as love. In a mature relationship there must always be a genuine self-giving that will "impress on love the invaluable mark of altruism" (p. 127). But the "concupiscible attitude" that emerges so quickly from sensual desire does not permit love to evolve into an interpersonal union where a couple strives for the other's good. In the relationship between Sharon and the mechanic, love failed to crystallize because there was no chastity to shield each of them from this concupiscence. Love cannot flourish in the face of excessive passion or emotional self-absorption that makes us oblivious to the person and his or her true good. Only the discredited virtue of chastity enables us to consistently affirm the value of the person and realize love's "true essence" (p. 128).

## Concupiscence of the flesh

Although sensuality constitutes the raw material for conjugal love, it is also associated with concupiscence of the flesh, which means that it can be the raw material for sin. Sensuality is the experience of the corporeal sexual values of another person. At this level there is a passive interest or "absorption" in sexual values that directs us to another person. The interest can quickly turn into desire as something in a person begins to strive for or "gravitate" toward those values (p. 130). At the stage of desire, the person affected by sexual values more actively turns to the bearer of those values and seeks him (or her) out. Sensual desire does not yet reach the threshold of willing, "but clearly tries to become it" (p. 130). When desire is not moderated but manages to impose itself on the will, the result is carnal or bodily love, which deliberately seeks enjoyment and satisfaction in the "body and sex" (p. 131). The possibility of these rapid transformations underscores the power of sensual desire, which conceals itself behind sensuality.

Thus, concupiscence of the flesh can pass from interest to desire, and from desire to willing, whereby one gives into his desires and deliberately seeks an outlet in bodily love. Concupiscence of the flesh pulls one toward a human being of the opposite sex; it proceeds in the direction of satisfying sexual desire, but once that desire is satisfied, "the entire relation to the object of desire breaks off" (pp. 131–132). For example, one man might find that his sexual *interest* in an attractive co-worker eventually leads to a strong sexual *desire*. But he overcomes these errant desires and finds ways to avoid the woman so he will not give in to his weakness. Thanks to his temperance, there is no transition to the next stage of *willing* or a deliberate attempt to initiate an illicit sexual relationship with her. Another colleague, however, has the same desires for this woman and he doesn't control them. So he willfully chooses to seduce her in order to indulge his lust. In the latter case, concupiscence of the flesh has induced this man's will (with his free cooperation) to pursue a temporary relationship with the woman, which is based on use for the sake of pleasure.

Carnal or bodily love born of uncontrolled concupiscence substitutes "the body and sex" for the whole person (p. 132). The body is detached from the person, and so it is no longer the means of giving to another, a medium for expressing commitment and contributing to the other's good, which is the essence of love. Rather, the body becomes "a 'terrain' of appropriation of the other person."[4] Concupiscence impels us toward physical intimacy. But if that intimacy is based solely on errant sexual desire, it does not have the value of a personal union. Hence it is the "denial of the love of persons," since it rests on the impulse to enjoy and to take rather than to give and to receive (p. 133). A properly integrated sensuality, instead, is subservient to reason and subdued by the profound realism of virtue. This kind of sensuality opens the way for the body to be a means of self-giving in the sexual act. The body can then manifest deep spiritual devotion that affirms one's spouse for who she is.

---

4. John Paul II, *Man and Woman*, 234.

# Subjectivism and egoism

To some extent, affectivity can safeguard us from the concupiscence of the flesh. These emotions are on a higher plane because they react more to the whole human person of the opposite sex, not just that person's body as a possible object of enjoyment. But because affectivity tends to make us idealize others, it is not the full answer to the problem of concupiscence. Emotional sentiment fosters idealization, which evades the problem instead of confronting it. Affectivity is still only the material for love, and it does not on its own create "an adequately deep basis for the love of the person to crystallize" (p. 134). The development of love, which must be shielded from the excesses of carnal desire, depends far more heavily on the virtue of chastity than on affectivity. The danger always exists that concupiscence of the flesh will appropriate those emotions so that carnal or bodily love will be accompanied by "a certain measure of 'lyricism' proceeding from affectivity" (p. 134).

The reference to the emotions as a possible safeguard against carnal desire becomes a central point of reference in Wojtyła's rebuke of subjectivism, which denies that there are objectively valid moral norms. According to Wojtyła, it is affection more than anything else that introduces "a subjective moment into human love" (p. 135). Affection must be differentiated from affectivity. As explained in Chapter Six, affectivity is an emotional experience of values, such as femininity, connected with a person of the opposite sex. But affection is a broader category that involves the range of the emotions typically accompanying the romantic involvement of two persons. These affections are enhanced by the deeds or actions that flow from our sensual and affective reaction to a person of the opposite sex. The point is that unchecked emotions have a tendency to introduce an unstable element into love between two people. Wojtyła explains that there are two forms of subjectivism. The first is emotional subjectivism or "subjectivism of affection," which should be quite familiar to those who have followed the argument of this book thus far (p. 135).

It would, of course, be foolish to assert that love should lack any emotion—such love would be cool and aloof. The problem occurs when the emotions become excessive and disproportionate, interfering with our ability to choose responsibly, guided by the light of truth. In that situation, reason finds itself serving the emotions, and moral truth becomes determined by the quest for emotional satisfaction. As Wojtyła explains, "affection in a sense averts 'the gaze of truth' from what is objective in action," so that the person becomes absorbed in her feelings, which color the truth of the whole experience (p. 136). According to Saint Thomas Aquinas, when these emotional motivations dominate, "one judges something to be appropriate and good which one would not have so judged, but for the passion."[5] Affection possesses only a "subjective veracity," and this opens up a "wide gate" for the justification of amorous activities that are incompatible with love's essence (p. 136).

It is a short and easy road, therefore, from allowing the emotions to dominate (emotional subjectivism) to confusion about moral values (subjectivism of values). This is the second form of subjectivism. It means that the person and all the objective values or properties associated with that person become an opportunity for pleasure and delight. Accordingly, pleasure "becomes the only value and the complete basis of valuation" (p. 137). Led by the quest for pleasure, we do whatever feels good and pleasurable (like casual sexual activity), and whatever feels good must also be right. For example, Wanda might say to her parents, "Look, having sex with my boyfriend makes me feel so satisfied, so intimate with him, how could it possibly be wrong?" But just because an action "feels right" and provides pleasure, it doesn't necessarily follow that this action is actually good for Wanda or for her boyfriend.

When the emotions control the will, pleasure often becomes the supreme value and the measure of all other values. Charity or respect for the person yields to pleasure. Pleasurable and agreeable experiences, especially sexual experiences, give us emotional satisfaction so that the emotions govern one's behavior. This inevitably leads to a fixation on pleasure alone, because emotion is naturally biased toward pleasure. The "hedonization of love" is the last bitter fruit of subjectivism (p. 138). When pleasure becomes the primary objective, a man or woman will not hesitate to use the other as an embodied, sexual being in order to satisfy his or her libidinous desires.

---

5. Saint Thomas Aquinas, *Summa Theologiae*, I–II, q. 10, a. 3c.

Since subjectivism is inward-focused, it tends to pervert love, and it is "the ground upon which egoism develops" (p. 138). Subjectivism leads a person to become preoccupied with his or her own pleasure rather than concentrate on willing the other's good. Egoism or self-centeredness is hostile to love, because love in its essence is always oriented toward the true good and fulfillment of the other person. True love requires altruism and the gift of self. But the egoist is exclusively concerned with his own immediate good, which amounts to his pleasurable experiences. At best, the pleasure seeker aims for mutual sexual satisfaction, but the other's satisfaction never comes at the expense of one's own pleasurable sensations. Authentic reciprocity and interpersonal union are impossible. This combination of subjectivism and egoism enthrones pleasure as the summit of the moral life. But pleasure is not an intelligible good that can be willed for the other, because it is merely a subjective and ancillary good that may or may not "happen." One can only want the other's pleasure, and then "only 'on condition' of one's own pleasure" (p. 139).

There are two forms of egoism that exclude love. Sensual egoism strives for pleasure that is provided by erotic experiences linked with enjoying another's body. The second is the more subtle form of egoism, which Wojtyła calls "egoism of affections" (or emotions) (p. 141). In this case, emotion for its own sake becomes the center of attention and the goal of one's actions, while sensual pleasure remains in the background. Perhaps a man stays with a woman only because her company gives him a thrill, an emotional "high" that he doesn't get from other women. He has little concern for her well-being but only for the excitement her company brings. Virtual relationships in cyberspace might be a good example of emotional egoism. Two people link up on a social network to find romance online, and they begin to exchange titillating or sexually suggestive emails. This intangible connection, which sometimes becomes physical, gives both individuals a great deal of emotional satisfaction. In all cases of emotional egoism, pleasure is the final end as the person slavishly follows his emotions for the sake of pleasure. The other is reduced to an object who satisfies the emotional needs of my ego. Emotional excess, therefore, can easily become a source of unchastity in the relationship between a man and a woman, though in a different way from sensual egoism. In most of these cases, unceasing novelty becomes an unhealthy surrogate for romantic stability.

To avoid subjectivism a person must unite the subjective and objective profiles of love. Without cultivating friendship and benevolence as a complement to sensuality and affectivity, a couple cannot be protected from egoism in its various guises and the concomitant disintegration of love. Where egoism prevails, conjugal love cannot be directed at an enduring interpersonal union and the true good of the other.

## The structure of sin

This account of subjectivism and egoism vividly discloses the reality of sinful love. By now we know that sensuality and affectivity are not bad in themselves, because they can serve as the energy for a passionate and vigorous marital relationship. But they must become transformed into love and charity through the spiritual capacities of will and intellect. Without such integration, without subordination to the ethical component of love, they become the basic material for sin thanks to concupiscence. Wojtyła returns to the theme of concupiscence, which represents the dangerous tendency "to see the person of the other sex through the values of *sexus* alone as an 'object of possible use'" (p. 142). Thanks to concupiscence one does not desire a person for her intrinsic value and worth as a person, but one looks upon the individual as a potential object of use. In his theology of the body, the Pope explains that "concupiscence . . . pushes man toward the possession of the other as an object, pushes him toward 'enjoyment.'"[6] The duty of love must triumph over this "constant inclination only to 'use'" and enjoy (p. 143).

Nevertheless, concupiscence of the flesh itself is not a sin but the "germ" of sin. As soon as the will consents and the person indulges his or her concupiscent desires, it becomes sinful. From that point the sensual appetite is not something merely "happening" in man but something he is actively pursuing. Wojtyła follows the traditional philosophy of Saint Thomas Aquinas in his insistence that the source of sin is always

---

6. John Paul II, *Man and Woman*, 263.

at the level of our free will. Despite the power of concupiscence of the flesh, which has its own dynamic, Wojtyła avoids any suggestion of determinism. The will, guided by reason, must prevent the body and its sexual values from becoming merely the object of enjoyment.

At the same time, we must recognize that concupiscence of the flesh is the "hotbed of sin," always prodding the will to cross the threshold from desire to consent and action, even if that action is only interior at first (p. 145). While in theory we can distinguish between the sexual desires triggered by concupiscence and lustful choices consented to by the will, in practice it is difficult to draw the precise "boundary of sin" (p. 145). In establishing that boundary we must note the difference between the spontaneous reaction of sensuality, incipient sexual desire, and the conscious, voluntary choice to follow those desires. We must differentiate between "not willing" and "not feeling"—while there are always feelings that happen to us, each rational human person is in control of his or her will and the actions that result from deliberate choices (p. 146). When analyzing the structure of sin, therefore, we must not exaggerate the role of sensuality or concupiscence of the flesh.

Sin is often the byproduct of the perilous attitude of subjectivism that greatly contributes to the rationalization of immoral behavior. Subjectivism seduces us into embracing a false concept of love and an inversion of values. Subjectivism of affection (or emotional subjectivism) reduces love to a subjective or emotional state. As a result, love is no longer directed at a durable interpersonal union and the good of the other, since "this does not enter the field of vision of the will disposed subjectivistically toward affection alone" (p. 147). The value of the person becomes subordinate to one's affective disposition, to what makes someone feel good. If a sensual infatuation with a married woman gratifies John's emotions, then this infatuation, however tawdry it may seem, becomes acceptable behavior because it satisfies the subjective norm of emotional fulfillment. In this way, the authenticity of feeling "becomes the enemy of truth in conduct" (p. 147).

As we have seen, subjectivism of affection leads inevitably to subjectivism of values. When our motivations are directed by the emotions rather than reason, we have a stronger tendency to accept the proposition: "whatever is pleasant must be good," since pleasure is so emotionally satisfying. Pleasure is thought to be the source of happiness, and the will focuses on pursuing pleasure as the highest good. These interrelated forms of subjectivism open the door for "sinful love," which occurs when there is no further development of sensual love and a couple willfully indulges their sexual desires. Wojtyła suggests that affectionate love can also be sinful if the partners treat each other as objects of enjoyment at an emotional level.

In sinful love that comes to pass from unchecked sensuality, a person is preoccupied with sensual enjoyment to the exclusion of the true good and valid needs of the other. Sinful love displaces care and affirmation of the person for his or her own sake with pleasure, as "delight connected with the sensory-sexual lived-experiences forces itself" into the relationship (p. 148). The body, dominated by lust, loses its capacity to express love and seeks only to appropriate another's body. One sees in the other only an attractive body isolated from the other as a person. The moral evil embodied in this sort of sin consists in "the fact that the person is treated as an 'object of use' or that both persons . . . treat each other in this way" (p. 148).

Sinful love is often deceptive. Although it has the outward appearance of love, it is only egoism and carnal desire in disguise, perhaps soothed by the emotional warmth of this provisional togetherness. Sinful love is the product of subjectivism, where a person is so absorbed in his emotional experience that the entire direction of his actions and choices is distorted. Strong emotions convey that this love is already fully mature, "that this is 'all' there is in love" (p. 149). Herein lies the real danger of sinful love: it is experienced by the human subject as love and not as something harmful and potentially destructive. But true love is willing the good of the other, which is neither affection nor sensual pleasure for its own sake. These are only secondary or accidental goods that do not contribute to human flourishing. It is impossible to build and sustain a durable union based on pleasure or emotional indulgence. The will, inspired by "the true vision of love," must protect the person from the destructive forces of subjectivism and egoism that dissolve and negate human love (p. 150). For this task, the will needs the help of virtues such as chastity.

# The true meaning of chastity

This extended treatment of concupiscence, egoism, and sinful love establishes the foundation for Wojtyła's presentation on the full sense or true meaning of chastity. When the objective truth about love is accepted, the virtue of chastity will be given the full respect it deserves. Those who appreciate the value of genuine love will recognize chastity as a "great positive factor of human life," a manifestation of the "culture of the person" that first takes shape in our interior life (p. 151).

Wojtyła again insists that love is complete only when it includes the virtue of charity (or benevolence) and a committed moral unity of friendship. Love as charity and binding commitment must be united with the psychological forces of sensuality and affectivity. This ensures that a relationship conforms with the personalistic norm. The psychological state of love is appealing, but it does not exhibit the "ethical essence of 'loving'" (p. 151). Chastity is essential in order to realize that essence, but what exactly is the full and proper sense of chastity?

Chastity has been traditionally linked with the cardinal virtue of temperance. A temperate person will control his desires for pleasure, especially the pleasures of sex, food, and drink. Temperance entails the power to restrain the "concupiscible impulses" that arise when sexual values impose themselves on our senses (p. 152). When temperance assumes this role of dealing with sexual pleasures (as opposed to other pleasures), it is commonly referred to as chastity. But proficiency or mastery does not represent the full meaning of chastity.

How then should we understand chastity's true nature? Wojtyła insists that rather than look for the essence of chastity in moderation, we must emphasize the natural affinity between chastity and love. The role of chastity is not just to ensure moderation but to free love from the utilitarian attitude that sanctions using another person for pleasure. Chastity's role is to "liberate love from the attitude to use" (p. 154). This utilitarian attitude derives not only from concupiscence, but even more from subjectivism and egoism that become the ingredients of sinful love, which often has the appearance of real love.

Chastity must not only control concupiscence of the flesh but also contend with "those interior centers in man from which the attitude to use emerges and spreads" (p. 154). Wojtyła means that the virtue of chastity is needed to help reason from falling under the sway of emotions. That condition leads to emotional subjectivism, which sees pleasure as the highest value and the only scale by which to measure other values. A man with this attitude to use will see only a woman's body and its sexual values rather than the whole person who manifests her inner self in and through that body. Chastity helps reason to preserve its control over sensuality and the concupiscible powers. Then reason can grasp the good of the whole person. Thus it opens the way for moral commitment and ultimately the total sharing that is characteristic of spousal love. Sensuality and affectivity severed from reason cannot see the good of the person and are more inclined to lust and domination. The virtue of love as willing the other's good requires such rational self-control. Chastity, therefore, helps a person cultivate a proper attitude toward the other person. Chastity prevents objectification by keeping sensuality and sentiment in their proper place so that they do not overwhelm reason and will.

Far from being inimical to love, chastity is a necessary condition of love. In Wojtyła's view, chastity means a "'transparency' of interiority" without which love cannot be itself (p. 154). Through that transparency the lover recognizes the other as a person and accepts the need to subordinate pleasure to the loving-kindness the person deserves. The chaste lover sees through the fog of passion and emotion so that his or her attention becomes properly focused on the other person's true good. The essence of chastity consists in this habitual readiness to affirm the value of the person in every context and to elevate to the personal level all sensual or sentimental reactions. Chastity, therefore, is primarily affirmative, not negative and repressive. It is first and foremost a saying "yes" to the dignity and value of the person. The virtue of chastity is threatened when someone discounts the value of the person and allows himself to be overwhelmed by sexual values. The true nature of chastity lies exactly "in 'keeping up' with the value of the person in every situation" (p. 155).

A chaste life is not a passive one, devoid of all passion and sexual vitality. Rather, a chaste life is one in which a man and a woman actively pursue the goods of friendship and spousal love. Without chastity's help, a man and a woman in a sexual relationship are vulnerable to becoming depersonalized *objects* in each other's eyes instead of *free gifts.* Hence, "only a chaste woman and a chaste man are capable of true love," for chastity frees their relationship from the tendency to use another person as an object, which is incompatible with loving-kindness (p. 156).

The temptation for young lovers is to identify love with spontaneous sensual desire and the emotional intensity that often accompanies it. "Burdened with concupiscence of the flesh," immature lovers locate love's essence in the satisfaction of those desires (p. 156). But mature lovers savor chaste loving, which is not devoid of sexual pleasure but of the attitude to use. Chaste love always affirms the value of the other person for his or her own sake. This love comes to fruition in a lifelong marriage in which a couple thrives and flourishes in the warmth and sexual intimacy of each other's company.

Chastity does not lead to disdain for the body, as some have erroneously supposed. It does mean that the body must be duly chastened in the face of the "greatness" represented by personhood. Through reason and virtue the humble body learns to subordinate carnal desire to true love. Accordingly, the body refuses to "subject love to itself" by aiming at sexual satisfaction at the expense of the value of the person (p. 157). The body must also humble itself before human happiness, since happiness is far more than the delights provided by the body and sexual activity. Rather, happiness is found in the "durable union" of marriage and intimate human exchange with a "personal character" (p. 157).

# Metaphysics of shame

The virtue of chastity is realized through shame and abstinence. Both "components" fortify and express this disposition to affirm the value of the person in our interactions with those of the opposite sex. Wojtyła's comprehensive treatment of shame anticipates the theology of shame presented in his theology of the body. There he describes shame as a necessary disposition to deal with our fallen sexual nature and our inclination to see the body as an object of enjoyment. Shame itself occurs when something of a private nature somehow becomes public against our wishes. Wojtyła concentrates on sexual shame or physical shame whose focus is the parts and organs of the body, which "determine its sexual distinctness" (p. 159). People have a natural tendency to conceal these parts from others and to avoid nakedness of the body in front of members of the opposite sex. Yet nakedness should not be identified with shamelessness. People in tropical climates with diverse cultural mores have a different attitude about nakedness, which does not imply sexual immodesty. Shame is not necessarily about the need to clothe one's private parts. Rather, the essential feature of shame is the tendency "to conceal the sexual values themselves" insofar as they become for a person of the opposite sex a potential object of enjoyment (p. 160).

Shame arises when the person recognizes that his or her body is vulnerable to manipulation for another's pleasure. As a result, human beings exhibit a strong inclination to conceal their sexual organs from the gaze of others. Men and women are naturally inclined to protect themselves against the prurient behavior of others, that is, against being regarded as an object of pleasure. However, since sensuality is more powerful in men, there is a greater need for modesty and shame in women in order to avoid enticing men into looking upon their bodies as objects for use. According to Wojtyła, "a man does not have to fear feminine sexuality as much as a woman must fear the masculine one" (p. 161). Men are keenly aware of their sensuality and this too is a source of shame, because a man is ashamed of the way he reacts to the sexual values of a woman. Wojtyła concludes that shame has two forms: shame as *relative*—that is, as a response to someone else's sensual reaction to my body as an object of use—and shame as "*immanent*," the need to prevent such concupiscent reactions in oneself to another's body because they are incompatible with the value of the person (p. 161). Shame gives rise to modesty, which is the tendency to avoid shameless behavior. The first form of shame is more relevant for women, who have a greater need to mollify aggressive male sensuality.

As an example let's consider Kathy, who was accustomed to wearing beautiful but somewhat immodest dresses in the office where she worked as a skilled paralegal. When a new co-worker named Dan arrived, Kathy noticed him glaring at her all the time; Dan also made sexual innuendos that made her feel uncomfortable. As a result of Dan's prurient looks and suggestive comments, Kathy became more vigilant about the way she dressed as a way of protecting herself from Dan. She began to wear more modest looking clothing that didn't repress her feminine beauty. Her hope was that this type of clothing would invite Dan to see her as more than a beautiful body. Kathy's behavior captures what Wojtyła means by *relative shame*. If Dan realizes that his disordered inclinations are the source of a pronounced change in Kathy's demeanor, he might feel mortified by his own behavior, and this represents *immanent shame*.

The natural tendency to protect the "sexual values" associated with the various parts of the human body reveals how sexual morality derives from the nature of personhood. Each person is by nature a self-possessing, self-governing being. No person wants to be taken possession of against her will, even if this "possession" occurs only in someone else's fantasies. The experience of shame is a reflection of the person's essential nature, "a natural resonance of what the person simply is" (p. 162). Only a person can feel shame, which to some extent has its origins in the "supra-utilitarian" character of the person. Shame arises because persons are inviolable, self-possessing beings who naturally defy objectification. Thus, Wojtyła refers to the need for a "metaphysical interpretation" of shame, because shame actually reveals the nature of the person as a being who belongs to herself. Moreover, the common experience of a woman's shame and indignation over a man's lustful look seems to confirm Wojtyła's theory of sexual morality predicated on the personalistic norm. As we have demonstrated, that theory assumes that the mature person strongly resists being treated as an object rather than being affirmed for her own sake.

Sexual modesty, which arises from the feeling of shame, is a natural form of self-defense. It safeguards the dignity of the person and preserves her status as a being who deserves to be free of sexual manipulation. Modesty helps to protect the person from the temptations derived from subjectivism so that true love can develop. A woman who dresses modestly shields herself from the lustful gaze of men and encourages them to respond to her with kindness and respect instead of lust. But shame and modesty are more than just a defensive mechanism. This retreat from another's reaction to my sexual values goes hand in hand with the aspiration to inspire love, that is, to inspire "a 'reaction' to the value of the person," which is the pathway to true love (p. 163). The concealing of sexual values is consistent with the status of the person as a superior being, who, unlike all other earthly creatures, is not made for use or enjoyment at the hands of another. Shame does not reveal the person in some abstract way, since people deeply feel their inviolability and independence. In response to a lustful glance, a woman may think, "You must not touch me," not even in your secret carnal thoughts and desires (p. 164). This fear of contact even through another's lustful thoughts affirms the dignity of the person, who resists being reduced to his or her attractive body.

Shame, however, is "absorbed" or swallowed up by love, though this does not imply that it is eliminated or destroyed. By "absorption" Wojtyła simply means that love puts shame to use for its own good purpose, so that it can keep in view the proper relationship between sexual values and the value of the person. Where there is love and affirmation of the person, there is no threat of selfish using or objectification. Shame then "loses its objective *raison d'être*" and recedes (p. 167). True conjugal love, which always includes charity and exclusive commitment, can absorb shame. Such love ensures that our sensual and emotional experiences are fully imbued with affirming the value of the person. Affirmation permeates consciousness along with the will's movements as it collaborates with the intellect so that the will is not threatened by the utilitarian attitude. Once someone realizes that his or her lover cares about his or her true good and welfare, there is no reason for shame, no reason for concealing the sexual values that can obscure the value of the person.

## The problem of shamelessness

In light of this account of shame, Wojtyła briefly treats the problem of shamelessness, which refers to the absence or negation of shame. Shame is a specific defense of the person who recoils from being treated as an object of use rather than an object of love. Shamelessness "destroys this whole order" of things, because it promotes the priority of lust over love (p. 172). Shamelessness can assume two forms: physical and emotional. Those culpable of physical shamelessness do not hesitate to display their bodies in sexually provocative ways that actually encourage objectification. A shameless woman, for example, deliberately tries to stir up the lustful feelings of a man. On the other hand, emotional shamelessness means that a person has no sense of shame or disgrace for his lust toward another, whom he sees as an object for sexual conquest. Emotional shame is not prudery, but a healthier reaction against disregarding this woman's irreducible value as a person.

Both forms of shamelessness are found in the contagion of pornography and in certain types of erotic art that accentuate the sexual element when depicting the human body. It thereby encourages viewers to fixate on a person's sexual attributes at the expense of the person herself. But more mundane forms of shamelessness abound, such as carelessness about the use of sexually suggestive attire. Within our sexualized culture, the attitude of shamelessness is reflected in a lack of modesty about the way men and women dress. Dress often highlights a person's sexual values, such as a woman's physical appearance, and there is nothing wrong with this so long as it is done with gracefulness and modesty. The problem arises, however, with a deliberate obfuscation of the value of the person. There is nothing shameful if Jane wants to look attractive for her boyfriend. But if she wears immodest and skimpy clothing that will make her look "hot" or "sexy" so she can arouse her boyfriend's feelings, her behavior is a form of shamelessness.

On the other hand, modesty is essential because men and women are not so "perfect" that they can always look at the sight of someone of the opposite sex in a disinterested way. When a woman dresses immodestly, her body can easily arouse concupiscence, a wish to enjoy that is concentrated on sexual values "while disregarding the essential value of the person" (p. 174). Modesty forestalls the threat of depersonalization that shrouds the significance of the person. Modesty thereby opens the way for the body to become an expression of love that speaks the language of the spirit.

Wojtyła's extensive treatment of shame is rather novel because it regards shame in a positive light, not as something to be dismissed for the sake of a more progressive attitude about sexuality. Shame has nothing to do with repression of legitimate sexual desire or a depreciation of human sexuality. Rather, shame is inspired by the need for a vigorous defense against the lustful advances of others. It also helps to curb those advances before they can lead to serious transgressions. Shame, therefore, serves the person by ensuring that sexual values do not eclipse the supreme value of personhood.[7]

# Problems of abstinence

## Moderation

The second ingredient of chastity is self-mastery or moderation, which allows a person to resist the pull of concupiscence. For Wojtyła, the chaste man is always the self-possessed man, who masters concupiscence of the flesh. A person must control concupiscence when it demands satisfaction in defiance of what reason recognizes as the right course of action. Blindly following one's libido might lead to a sexual union, but a union that is based on indifferent self-centeredness. The temperate or moderate person acts honorably and reasonably, always in a manner worthy of a mature self-possessed being. Failure to achieve self-mastery jeopardizes a person's ability to transcend herself so that she can become a gift for others. The philosopher Jacques Maritain often spoke about the need for self-mastery as a condition for the spiritual existence of self-giving.[8]

Thus, control of concupiscence is essential not only for a person's moral perfection but for a realization of love in the world of persons. A person must moderate both physical desires and the emotions that often accompany them. When those sub-rational desires are out of control, the person is likely to retreat from responsible moral action. But the moderate person acts and desires well. By moderation, Wojtyła means the capacity to avoid excess, to find the middle ground in the command of our "sensual excitability and affective sensibility" that will enable us to realize true romantic love and avoid the danger of exploitation (p. 179). The life of moderation or temperance is the life of balance

---

7. See Grondelski, "Fiftieth Anniversary of *Love and Responsibility*," 27.

8. Jacques Maritain, *Challenges and Renewals* (Notre Dame: Notre Dame University Press, 1966), 75.

and measure. Although moderation means self-mastery, it should not mean that one is confined to a life of mediocrity devoid of sensual desire. Rather, moderation implies "the ability to maintain equilibrium among the movements of the concupiscence of the flesh" (p. 180).

A person who fails to attain self-mastery in the sexual sphere is not self-possessed and cannot be chaste. Instead he or she is "possessed" by those intense desires that control the will. Wojtyła describes this "interior situation" in which a person defends himself against the "invasion" of errant desires that come from concupiscence of the flesh (p. 180). The morally responsible person recognizes the threat to his natural powers of self-determination. His freedom is at stake, and it cannot be preserved unless he finds a way to transcend these desires in favor of the true moral good.

So the virtue of moderation or temperance is expressed in terms of self-mastery in the sexual sphere. Without self-mastery, which ensures rational self-governance, a person cannot be chaste. And the method for achieving self-mastery is continence, "the habit of restraining the concupiscence of the flesh by the will" (p. 181).

Continence or abstinence, however, should never be an end in itself. Continence, the habit of resisting sexual impulses, does not yet "determine the full realization of virtue" (p. 181). On the contrary, continence becomes a virtue only when it is practiced for a noble end: safeguarding another person from being exploited and used for pleasure. Virtuous behavior requires recognition of and deference to the value of the person, which always takes precedence over sexual values. When the value of the person "'takes the lead' in the whole lived-experience . . . continence is not 'blind' anymore" (p. 182). Rather, continence becomes the means for realizing this higher value. It is not enough to restrain sexual desires, for man must know exactly *why* he restrains them. The "why" is as important as the "how." When continence is practiced for the sake of the objective value of personhood, it "acquires the meaning of a fully-mature virtue" (p. 183). This is what Wojtyła means by the subordination of continence to the process of "objectivization." In the midst of sexual attraction and desire, the *objective* value or intrinsic worth of the person must enter our consciousness and "take command" of what is happening at the sensory and emotional level. A person must understand that self-restraint is necessary to protect the other person and preserve the personal dignity of the body. Deference to this ultimate moral value of embodied personhood calms the will and liberates it from a sense of loss.

For example, consider a man who walks into a local pub known for its reputation as a singles bar. He starts to talk with a strikingly beautiful and vulnerable woman, who is quite open to his flirtations. If he is an immoderate and unchaste man, he will give free reign to that "look of concupiscence" so that he comes to see the woman primarily as a body to be used for his enjoyment. But if he is a chaste and virtuous man, he will exercise self-control and moderate his sexual desires. He will do this not for the sake of self-restraint for its own sake, but because he sees this woman as a person who is called to a real communion of persons and whose true good is not objectification through casual sex with him. The man may have some regrets over this lost opportunity, but such regret is mitigated by the realization that his restraint has conserved the woman's dignity along with his own integrity.

Thus, the virtue of chastity depends on the direction of reason that keeps this vision of the whole person in close view. Reason is persuasive, not blindly coercive. It is always sensitive to the beauty of well-ordered sensuality as well as the body's tendency to use another in defiance of the personalistic norm. Wojtyła displays remarkable wisdom in these passages since he knows that continence is quite difficult for many people. Yet they will better respond to the challenge of controlling their sexual impulses if they see that it is for a laudable purpose: to safeguard the dignity of the person and to open up the possibility of love instead of use.

Affectivity or emotional sentiment can also play a supporting role in this process, because the person's value "should not be only 'coldly' understood, but also felt" (p. 184). The value of the person as a self-possessing and morally independent being ultimately has a metaphysical connotation that does not generate much feeling. But an emotional affinity for the value of the person can develop with the support of affectivity, a spontaneous reaction to another's masculinity or femininity. If affectivity's tendency to idealize these values is linked with an intellectual recognition of the value of the person, the virtue of chastity secures crucial support "in the emotional sphere" (p. 185). Wojtyła means that affectivity is the source of emotional devotion, and it often prompts us to put the beloved on a pedestal. This is fine so long as our primary motivation is to affirm the person for his or her own sake and to protect the person from being used.

The notion of emotional support for the virtue of chastity is consistent with Wojtyła's firm conviction that affectivity and sensuality invigorate love. They must be controlled but not repressed. A person should strive to use these dynamic energies with "some diplomacy" so that they become "allies in pursuing true love" instead of its foes (p. 185). The proficiency for transforming potential enemies into allies is an essential characteristic of the virtue of chastity.

## Tenderness and sensuality

As he concludes this chapter, Wojtyła briefly addresses the issue of tenderness and its link to sensuality. Tenderness grows from affectivity but performs a specific function in human life. We feel tenderness for a person when we become conscious of that person's connection with us in a certain way. Tenderness represents our inclination to empathize with another's inner feelings such that they become our own. But tenderness is more than empathy or some sort of commiseration. Tenderness is the propensity "to embrace the other's lived-experiences and the states of the other person's soul with one's own affection" (p. 186). Thanks to tenderness, a friend or spouse feels what I feel and is willing to suffer or rejoice on my behalf. Supported by affective commitment, tenderness creates intimacy that has a need to communicate itself. Therefore, tenderness naturally expresses itself through exterior displays of affection. But the core of tenderness is always found within the person, for tenderness is something "personal, interior, one's own" (p. 187).

The problem with tenderness from a moral viewpoint is that it can be clothed with sexual connotations. However, tenderness should always be differentiated from sensuality, which is oriented toward the body's sexuality. Tenderness is not an expression of concupiscence but of benevolence and personal devotion. Thus tenderness should never be confused with the need to satisfy sensuality. Unlike sensuality, tenderness is "marked by a regard for the other," although it need not be completely disinterested (p. 188). Tenderness can be accompanied by a need to satisfy one's own affectivity, and this can bring about an intimacy or closeness between two people. Tenderness, therefore, must be properly cultivated and controlled so that it does not assume a different meaning and become an outlet for the satisfaction of sensual desire. Sincere displays of tenderness that emanate from a devoted commitment and care for a person of the opposite sex always require a certain vigilance.

Since tenderness can sometimes devolve into indiscreet behavior or even sexual use, it needs the support of chastity and self-mastery so that it can serve love rather than hinder it. Tenderness is a salient feature of love because love thrives on affection and signs of affection. The "constant contribution of affection" creates an atmosphere of reciprocal understanding so each member of a couple feels "at home" and at ease with the other (p. 191). When combined with real love for a spouse, tenderness is capable of preserving love from the dangers of egoism or emotional indifference. Marriage devoid of tenderness becomes cold and dispassionate. Where tenderness abounds so too does the conviction that one is not alone, and with that conviction comes a heightened "consciousness of union" (p. 192).

It may seem odd to address the topic of tenderness in the context of a discussion on abstinence. But true tenderness, like love, requires a will committed to mature continence that overcomes a utilitarian attitude, which regards other persons as objects of use for pleasure. Affectivity, which often gives birth to tenderness, can be "'material' for egoism" as well as for love (p. 192). Affectivity and empathy can become an excuse for seeking deeper intimacy through sexual relations. Therefore, we must be on guard against spurious forms of tenderness, which only cloak the "egoism that contradicts love" (p. 192). Authentic tenderness creates an opportunity for romantic love to flourish into spousal love. Abstinence plays a critical role in all this, because it ensures that sensuality and affectivity do not get in the way of love's proper expression and development.

## Summary

Chastity is the virtue that enables us to contend with concupiscence, which represents the evolution of sensuality from interest to desire. When desire is uncontrolled by the will, the result is sinful love. Subjectivism, which posits pleasure as the supreme value, gives concupiscence free reign within the soul and eventually leads to egoism, where pleasure is selfishly pursued at the expense of another person's dignity.

But the virtue of chastity frees us from concupiscence and lustful temptations in order to enable an authentic and loving personal union based on self-giving. Without chastity, "The body is left as an object of concupiscence and thus as a 'terrain of appropriation' of the other human being."[9] Chastity is the spiritual strength that sustains an interior transparency within existing or potential sexual relationships. Chastity enables us to see and affirm the other always as a person who deserves respect and loving-kindness. Chastity is a virtue derived from reason's persuasive capacity to give priority to the value of personhood over sensuality and emotional sentiment, without so denigrating these valuable dynamisms that they lose their efficacy as "allies" in the quest for love. Through the disquieting feeling of shame a person shields herself from the concupiscent look of another person. Through self-mastery and moderation, the person relies on abstinence when necessary to affirm with feeling and warmth the intrinsic value of the other person in every stage of a maturing sexual relationship. Thanks to chastity, a man and a woman are capable of the reciprocal self-gift and personal communion that comes to fruition in marriage. The virtues of chastity and love, therefore, are interdependent and condition one another.

Wojtyła's main task is almost accomplished. He has convincingly presented the case for why the self-possessing person deserves to be loved and not used, and he has demonstrated the essential qualities of love. The nobler elements of love include benevolence, willing the other's good, and the committed union of friendship. Spousal love is the highest form of love and manifests itself in total reciprocal self-donation. Love is enhanced by sensuality and affectivity, which are the raw material for conjugal love. Several conditions are necessary for living out spousal love as a virtue. For example, spousal love must always be freely

---

9. John Paul II, *Man and Woman*, 260.

chosen. Freedom depends on the ability to rise above the emotions and sensuality to commit to another based on the truth of his or her value as a person, and on whether or not he or she is a fitting soul mate for me. True love, however, is endangered by concupiscence and carnal desire, which lead to sinful love if they overtake the will. Hence true love based on freedom needs the virtue of chastity, the disposition to always see the dignity and value of the person without the distortions created by sensual desire. Where love flourishes thanks to chastity, there will be no objectification but a unification and an enriched self-possession, the fruit of self-donation. What remains to be considered are the features of marriage, which institutionalizes spousal love for this life of mutual self-donation.

------- Chapter 9 -------

# Marriage

## *(Chapter IV: Part One)*

In the subtle and appealing opening scene of *The Jeweler's Shop*, Andrew asks Theresa to marry him by saying, "Do you want to be my life's companion?" She explains how Andrew spoke these words as he peered ahead into the distance, "as if to signify that in front of us was a road whose end could not be seen."[1] This unconventional proposal surprised Theresa, but she knew exactly what Andrew meant and she graciously consented to be his wife.

Spousal love is a lifelong, exclusive companionship that involves total union and mutual sharing "closely linked to the bodily . . . existence of man" (p. 196). Sexual difference makes possible this intimate unity of spousal love, which bears fruit in the generation of new life. Every person achieves fulfillment and perfection in self-donation, and this form of love is the exemplary way for two human persons to give themselves to one another.

Spousal love needs an "appropriate framework" that will ensure the full development of the sexual relationship and the durability of

---

1. Wojtyła, *The Jeweler's Shop*, Act 1, Scene 4.

interpersonal union (p. 195). That framework, of course, is marriage. As we have already seen, marriage is unique among human relationships because spousal love is based on sexual reciprocity, which essentially implies fruitfulness. Every human person exists as a masculine or feminine being and has a natural yearning for a person of the opposite sex to complement one's life. This limitation or dependency is confirmed by the fact that human beings are incomplete in respect to sexual reproduction, which can occur only when a man and woman unite organically. Their two bodies become "one flesh" (Gn 2:24) when they are biologically united in this way. Marital love represents the union between two persons of different sexes that is open to a third person.[2] Thus, the structure and purpose of marriage is derived from its innate orientation to procreation, which is absent in other human relationships. Because procreation is the "principal end" of marriage, it has a unique and unchangeable "inter-personal structure" (p. 201). Marriage, therefore, is not a malleable institution nor an arbitrary social construct, but a natural and moral reality.[3]

## Monogamy and indissolubility of marriage

Like all human relationships, marriage is subject to the personalistic norm. It follows from this norm and the nature of spousal love that marriage must be supported by two fundamental moral principles: exclusivity and indissolubility. Jesus himself expressed this mandate with unmistakable clarity, and emphasized that this arrangement was the original plan of the Creator (see Mt 19:4–6; Mk 10:2–9). The personalistic norm assuredly confirms his teaching. That universal moral norm, which "dwells" within the command to love and can be comprehended by "reason alone," invites us to exhibit loving-kindness and to always treat persons in a manner proper to their nature (p. 197). Both

---

2. Scola, *Nuptial Mystery*, 132.

3. In this discussion on marriage I have relied on the extremely helpful insights of Sherif, Girgis, Robert George and Ryan Anderson, *What Is Marriage? Man and Woman: A Defense* (New York: Encounter Books, 2012).

polygamy and the dissolubility of a valid marriage clash with the demands of the personalistic norm. Marriage is always meant to be a lasting and exclusive companionship, two people embarking on a journey "whose end could not be seen."[4]

Marriage is indissoluble because if love is based on the value of the person, it will last forever. When man and woman unite in conjugal love, the love continues until one spouse is no longer alive. The marriage bond ends at death because this union is a "bodily and earthly one" (p. 196). The subjective feelings of a married couple may change, but this cannot alter the objective reality of their commitment and their moral unity as man and wife. A dissoluble or provisional arrangement, on the other hand, creates many opportunities for one member of a married couple to be treated opportunistically by another. Spouses should not be abandoned, because desertion treats them as if they were disposable things rather than persons. Love is a moral commitment and a promise. In the case of spousal love, that commitment is forever binding and cannot be withdrawn. To sanction such withdrawal is to undermine the very essence of spousal love. Marriage has certain essential features, such as permanence and exclusivity, because the goods of marriage and parenthood cannot be suitably realized without them. Without permanence, there is neither reliability nor the peace and joy that are "closely linked to [love's] very essence" (p. 70). We cannot accept that a marital union is contingent on the psychological states of sensuality and affectivity, which ebb and flow during a relationship. To base such a profound personal union on these unstable grounds would contradict the personalistic norm. A change of heart, then, cannot abolish the fact that a married couple who have had conjugal relations are "objectively united to each other" as spouses (p. 199).

In a fairly well-known romantic comedy, one of the characters tries to rationalize the breakup of his marriage. He complains that after a number of years his wife was losing her youthful beauty and becoming more melancholy. As a result, all his erotic interest in her has slowly evaporated. Yet, when his wife becomes sick, he dutifully takes care of

---

4. Wojtyła, *The Jeweler's Shop*, op. cit.

her for several years. On the brink of a messy divorce, his new girlfriend explains that he's "paid his dues" and now it's time to move on. In this man's view, marriage seems to be something primarily egocentric, with the main emphasis on the satisfaction of his personal needs. There is a commitment to the other, but that commitment is conditional and limited. Obviously, this is the wrong way to see spousal love, which is selfless, unconditional, and permanent. It is focused on the union or connection between husband and wife, with each member of the couple devoted to the other's good. To be sure, this love is burdened by the hard realities of married life, but through grace and sincere effort those burdens can be surmounted.

Marital love is also monogamous or exclusive because the union of man and woman is a full and complete union based on the gift of one's whole self. There is no possibility for another union of the same sort at the same time. The human self is indivisible, so a person cannot divide herself and give herself exclusively and totally to several different partners. The human soul simply has no room for multiple spouses. Moreover, polygamy usually leads to men treating women as objects of enjoyment. Polygamous relationships implicitly regard persons of the other sex as objects that represent only a sexual value or a means to procreation. Monogamy, on the other hand, underscores the value of the person as the exclusive focus of marital love over the power of sexual values, which have their own immediacy. Without exclusivity and fidelity, the trust proper to a marital relationship can never be sustained. Instead of consolation and security, feelings of jealousy and betrayal will arise.

To uphold the principles of monogamy and indissolubility clearly requires the integration of romantic love with the ethical requirements of love as a virtue. The need for this integration implies that a man and a woman must have a mature love before their marriage takes place, where friendship and benevolence have had sufficient time to develop. Friendship itself is already a moral commitment that is deepened in the marital covenant. Love must be mature enough "for further maturation within marriage and through marriage" (p. 199).

The objective moral order is preserved in principle by strict monogamy, which also includes indissolubility. Although this high standard is at the heart of marriage, it is difficult for some people to accept. The reason for this hesitancy is that people too often mistake love in its subjective or strictly psychological sense with love in its full objective and ethical sense. As Wojtyła has been at pains to insist, conjugal love is not just sensuality and amorous sentiment, but a lasting, unconditional commitment to another person. If we accept Wojtyła's doctrine of conjugal love, love in its fullest sense, as mutual self-giving sealed by the conjugal act, a man and a woman complete each other in marriage to become a one-flesh union. They cannot separate without revoking their unconditional commitment and causing great damage to each other (and to their children), which is incompatible with the personalistic norm. Empirical studies of the trauma caused by divorce certainly provide ample evidence of this damage. Of course, marriage also demands permanence and exclusivity because it is naturally oriented to the generation and nurture of children, who need the stable environment provided by two committed parents.

## The value of the institution of marriage

Marriage is also an ethical and social institution, which means that it has been established according to the norms of justice. The social ramifications of sexual relations require the justification of this act through the institution of marriage. Sexual relations lead to children and to the institution of the family, in which every society has a certain stake. The family is a "small society" on which larger societies (such as the state or the Church) depend for their own ongoing vitality and stability. "It is understandable," writes Wojtyła, "that this large society tries to watch over the process of its continuous becoming through the family" (p. 201). The lack of a family does not deprive marriage of its true character as an enduring union of persons. But marriage exists to serve love, and marriage serves love more fully when it serves existence and becomes a family. As Wojtyła explains later in a papal letter titled *Familiaris Consortio*, love is a gift, and a married couple do not just give themselves to each other but they give the gift of existence to a new human person.[5] This generosity invigorates and sustains a marriage.

---

5. John Paul II, *Familiaris Consortio* (Boston: Pauline Books & Media, 1981), §3.

The public nature of marriage confirms its social significance. Marriage vows are exchanged in public before witnesses, who pledge to support the couple and to help them keep their wedding vows. The institution of marriage is necessary to protect marital norms such as monogamy and to signify the mature union between man and woman. The institution of marriage enables a man and a woman to publicly ratify their commitment. Marriage, therefore, justifies the sexual relationship between a certain couple in their eyes and in the eyes of society. The institution of marriage sends a strong signal about the importance of the marital relationship and invokes social pressures on preserving a couple's commitment.[6]

If promiscuity is easily tolerated, this justification will seem quaint and outdated. With its looser moral standards, contemporary Western culture has a far greater allowance for cohabitation and promiscuity. So the importance of marriage as a social institution has greatly diminished. Nonetheless, within a society "acknowledging healthy ethical principles and living in accord with them" without hypocrisy, the institution of marriage continues to signify the maturity of the union between a man and a woman (p. 204). When two people marry, they testify to others that their love is the foundation for a lasting union and a nurturing family life.

Sexual relations outside of marriage are always wrong, but adultery involving another person's husband or wife is especially grievous. Adultery involves a gross injustice as the adulterer seeks what is not his own. Marriage, therefore, serves another purpose because it creates proper boundaries and settles questions regarding the "reciprocal belonging of persons to each other" (p. 206). The institution of marriage justifies conjugal relations and signifies an enduring commitment. Without this institutional framework to support spousal love, the person can be more easily degraded in the sexual relationship to being an object of another's pleasure. Deliberate "free love," therefore, is always morally wrong because it represents a "rejection of the institution of

---

6. Elizabeth Brake, "Minimal Marriage: What Political Liberalism Implies for Marriage Law," *Ethics* 120 (2010), 332.

marriage" by reducing or undermining its role in the sphere of sexual relations (p. 206).

Sexual relations must be justified or "made just" not only in the eyes of society but in the eyes of God the Creator. Man is a creature who completely depends on the Creator. Thanks to his reasoning powers, man realizes that he is simultaneously his own property and, as a creature, he is also the property of the One who made him and sustains his existence. In marriage, a man and a woman become each other's property, but they are already God's property. If a couple accepts this "supreme right of ownership," they must seek justification before God for their sexual union whereby they give themselves to each other (p. 208). Hence the sacramental nature of marriage: the sacrament of nature, which is first introduced in Genesis as an institution ordained by the Creator, is reinforced in the Gospels by the sacrament of grace. In that sacrament the Creator approves and sanctions this reciprocal gift of self between two of his creatures. Only the sacrament of Marriage, which bestows graces on the couple and signifies God's approval of their union through his Church, justifies the marital relationship in God's eyes. These graces give married couples the strength to persevere in their exclusive and committed conjugal love.

# Reproduction and parenthood: justifying the sexual act

The institution of marriage forms the objective framework so that this "durable union of persons" can be realized based on the principles of indissolubility and monogamy (p. 210). Marriage justifies the sexual relationship between a man and a woman. Their sincere commitment, expressed in the exchange of marital vows, signifies that they are not using each other within a hedonistic relationship, but are cooperating with the Creator to create new persons and build a family. However, each sexual act also requires its own internal justification. Even within the context of marriage, sexual acts must be in conformity with the objective demands of the personalistic norm in order to avoid instrumentalizing the other person. In the marital act a couple must show responsibility for their love complemented by a responsibility for the basic goods of marital communion, including life-in-transmission. How can this responsibility be properly lived out?

As man and woman unite in a full sexual relationship, they freely project themselves into the "order of nature." This simply means that these two individuals must realize that the "natural finality" or purpose of their sexual activity is procreation, so they cannot use their sexual capacities in ways that deliberately thwart that purpose (p. 211). The conjugal act is not just a union of persons but a union of persons in relation to procreation. Thanks to their sexual union they have an opportunity to generate a new human life, a person who can become part of the human community. This is why the sexual drive has an existential significance: it points toward procreation, which is the beginning of the existence of the person, and that existence is the source of all other human perfections. Thus, when viewed objectively and honestly, marriage must be seen not just as an emotional bonding between two persons, but as a sexual and full personal union of a man and a woman that is affected by the possibility of procreation.[7]

However, since marriage involves two *persons* it is not merely about reproduction. In a morally suitable sexual relationship there is a fusion of the natural order and the personal order. The marital commitment is sealed and reinforced when man and woman freely join together in the generative act as an expression of their love and lasting commitment. A couple participates in the "natural order" by coming together as a one-flesh union with both bodies naturally striving for reproduction.[8] Thus, by engaging in the sexual act "they choose to participate in creating" (p. 213). The personal order finds expression in the exclusive intimacy and conscious self-surrender that takes place between two persons in the marital act. In the animal world only reproduction occurs. But among persons "the sexual drive, so to speak, enters the gates of consciousness and the will, providing not only the conditions of fertility but at the same time the specific 'material' for love" (p. 212). Conjugal love, therefore, is always oriented toward intimate union and the true good of the beloved.

---

7. See Edward Feser, *The Last Superstition* (South Bend, IN: St. Augustine's Press, 2010), 141–152.

8. Pruss, *One Body*, 146.

Some married couples seem hesitant to accept that their sexual activity projects them into the order of nature and endows the conjugal act with procreative meaning. However, when a man and woman freely choose to marry and have sexual relations, they choose at the same time the possibility of procreation, the opportunity to share in the creation of new human life. To be sure, because they are persons that act takes on another meaning as a manifestation of their total love and exclusive commitment. Thus, sexual relations are truly marital only when this organic bodily union aimed at procreation is linked with a free expression of exclusive and reciprocal self-giving. The marital act must always be generative in kind, even if it does not result in the generation of new life, *and* it must be an expression of spousal love.[9] The personal and natural orders cannot be separated. If marital intercourse is to be a total one-flesh union that allows a couple to experience itself as one, then contraception, which imposes barriers between a husband and wife, must be precluded. The use of a condom, for example, is an intentional act that strikes a direct blow against such a complete one-flesh union.

Given his interest in a person's whole interior life and self-experience, it is perhaps no surprise that Wojtyła focuses so intently on the interior dimensions of the marital act. In the sexual act, members of a married couple intend in their minds and hearts to fully give themselves to each other in this sexual union as a means of intensifying their spousal love and exclusive commitment. This total sharing and union, however, cannot exclude their fertility and potential parenthood. Hence the sexual act is justified only if there is an awareness and a willing acceptance that "'I can become a father' or 'I can become a mother'" (p. 214). The sexual union is fully elevated to a personal union only when "parental readiness is not positively excluded" (p. 215). Such readiness is so decisive that without it there can only be a mere sexual association rather than an interpersonal union.

What's the reasoning behind this declaration about the need for a willing acceptance of parenthood? Those who enter into marriage do so

---

9. See Girgis, George, and Anderson, *What Is Marriage?* and John Crosby, "Karol Wojtyła's Personalist Understanding of Man and Woman," in *Personalist Papers*, ed. John Crosby (Washington, D.C.: Catholic University of America Press, 2004), 243–263.

(or should do so) to become fathers and mothers, and when children come, they realize their vocation to parenthood, which is part of the marriage vocation. Children perfect the marital communion and enrich a couple's relationship. An unwillingness for parenthood, which is a repudiation of the marital calling, often leads to the deliberate steriliza-tion of sexual intercourse. This is wrong because by holding back their fertility, a married couple acts against the union their love seeks. The "one-flesh" union naturally strives for procreation and the fruitful gift of a child that is made possible by sexual reciprocity. Although the sexual act need not actually be fruitful each time it is undertaken, it cannot be forcefully detached from sexual fruitfulness. To do so by artificial means is to divide the married couple in two in the very act in which its pro-found unity is made most manifest.[10]

The contraceptive act also deprives a spouse of the chance to be a parent. This impoverishes the marital relationship, which cannot grow as an authentic community of persons. In this case, one or perhaps even both spouses are not willing the true good of the other, which is the opportunity for parenthood and family. As a result, love is not present in its fullness, and this impairs the personal relationship between a hus-band and wife. In one of his later essays, Wojtyła explains that the marital bond is brought to fruition by parenthood, and unwillingness for parenthood undercuts that fulfillment. According to Wojtyła, "Marriage as a *communio personarum* is by nature open to these new persons . . . a community that exists and acts on the basis of the bestowal of humanity and the mutual exchange of gifts."[11]

Wojtyła certainly realized that this doctrine would be mightily resisted. He himself later witnessed the resistance in the strident reac-tion to Pope Paul VI's encyclical *Humanae Vitae*. But this teaching must be seen in the light of the two critical principles that undergird the

---

10. G. Martelet, *Amour Conjugale et Renouveau Conciliare* (Lyon: Gaillard, 1969), 33. See Scola, *Nuptial Mystery*, 125. See also Germain Grisez, *Living a Christian Life* (Quincy, IL: Franciscan Press, 1993), 681–683. I have benefited greatly from Professor Grisez's elaboration on marriage and family in this treatise on Christian moral theology.

11. Karol Wojtyła, *Person and Community: Selected Essays*, trans. T. Sandok (New York: Peter Lang, 1993), 327.

arguments in *Love and Responsibility* and provide the framework for Wojtyła's theory of sexual morality: the natural purpose of our sexual capacities is procreation, and each person must be loved and not used as a mere means (the personalistic norm). Fidelity to both of these principles means that the only way to deal with the sexual drive is to use it for its natural purposes or to resist it. A couple that rejects the sexual drive's procreative purpose and uses these sexual powers only for pleasure and self-gratification ends up using each other.

But perhaps a married couple might object: "Yes, we reject the procreative purpose of our sexual powers but we engage in sexual relations to express our loving union, our exclusive self-donation, which is also essential to marriage." This would seem like a valid argument. However, their self-donation is not complete and total as it should be, but conditional. They do not give themselves fully to each other since they withhold their fertility and procreative capacity. Hence the marital act does not then express total and unconditional self-giving, and there is only a semblance of the comprehensive union that should characterize marital love. The self-centered concerns that have damaged this gift have opened the door to selfish using. With the possibility of children and parenthood negated and with no full union that signals each person's generosity, the sexual act is easily degraded to mutual pleasure seeking. The couple is more concerned with *"getting"* pleasure rather than *giving* their whole selves. As Wojtyła concludes, "man can remain faithful to the person in the order of love . . . insofar as he is faithful to nature" (p. 216). It is impossible to separate the personal and natural dimensions of marriage. We can't pretend that it's all about reproduction *or* that it's all about a personal union expressed in the sexual act and not about the fruitfulness of that act, which yields the goods of parenthood and new life.

The generosity signified by openness to new life enhances the marital union. It helps preserve it from devolving into an insular and self-centered relationship. Conscious acceptance of the possibility of parenthood helps to dissolve the casual egoism that can easily intrude upon sexual relations. Each person becomes more focused on the goods of parenthood and family for each other. Both persons in the marital union must "act in conformity with the interior logic of love; they respect the interior dynamic of love and open themselves to the new good, which in this case is an expression of the creative power of love" (p. 216). Sinful love is egoistic and fixated on pleasure. Real conjugal love, however, is expressed in a bodily interpersonal union where a couple generously extends a welcome hand to the new person whom that union may create. The attitude of parental readiness overcomes "bilateral egoism," behind which lies the use of persons (p. 216).

Wojtyła reiterates the claim made in earlier chapters that people have difficulty accepting the natural order, which they confuse with biology. This persistent confusion prevents them from seeing that the sexual drive is not just a biological force that can be manipulated for any purpose. Nature has ordained for us certain ends, and the end or purpose of our sexual powers is procreation. This order of nature has God as its author, and he expects us to engage in the sexual act in a way that conforms with its natural purpose. Hence we cannot act contrary to nature by obstructing the purpose of our sexual powers by contraception.

The common threat of subjectivism compounds the problem, because it induces married couples to mistake pleasurable erotic sensation for love. Erotic experiences can certainly enhance marital union, but not when they distract a couple from recognizing each other's value as a person. When pleasure becomes the exclusive goal, the sterilized sexual act is neither procreative nor expressive of committed conjugal love. Then the couple is using the sexual act for self-gratification rather than to reinforce the true good of marital fidelity, which is realized through a complete bodily union and a total sharing at all levels of their being. The value of the person can only be respected if the sexual act is in harmony with the natural purpose of marriage, and with no possibility of exploitation. According to Wojtyła, "the erotic lived-experiences connected with sexual intercourse of a man and a woman that positively exclude the parental moment . . . cancel the value of the person" (p. 217).

The conjugal act is a procreative act. If we pretend otherwise, we are deprived of a fruitful union of bodies that signifies the union of the whole person.[12] When parental readiness is categorically dismissed, the sexual act is stripped of the generosity proper to its nature and begins to devolve into self-centered using. The conjugal act is now corrupted by

---

12. Scola, *Nuptial Mystery*, 237–238.

selfishness, which weakens the bonds of this union and interferes with the affirmation of one's spouse as person and potential parent. Without the interior attitude of parental readiness, a couple is saying "I refuse to be a father" and "I refuse to be a mother," even though I engage in an act whose primary purpose is procreative. This refusal amounts to a living contradiction that can strike at the heart of a marriage.

The interior attitude of readiness for parenthood attains the right balance between overemphasis on procreation and its positive exclusion. In marriage one strives for interpersonal union along with the other's true good, which includes the goods of parenthood and family. However, this striving does not imply that the spouses "be required to positively will procreation in every act of intercourse" (p. 219). Such a position conceals a subtle form of utilitarianism because it implies that marital love is a means to an end. Sexual union is meant to express the total romantic union of two persons who are forever committed to each other. Thus, no couple should assume the role of "breeders" and perform the sexual act without the correct disposition for the sole purpose of producing a child. Conjugal love should be an "act of uniting persons, and not merely a 'tool' or 'means' of procreation" (p. 220).

At the same time, the positive exclusion of procreation also clashes with the proper character of conjugal intercourse. Accordingly, Wojtyła rejects any form of positive contraception whereby one intentionally acts to prevent sexual intercourse from resulting in reproduction.[13] In the case of the positive exclusion of the possibility of conception by means of contracepted intercourse, conjugal love is no longer directed to an unconditional interpersonal union and the good of the other. When a man and a woman positively exclude the possibility of motherhood and fatherhood, they turn away from each other's good and begin to focus on themselves and the pleasure they derive from sexual intercourse. Instead of persons being co-creators of love, they are partners in erotic experiences. Such a pleasure-centered orientation clearly contradicts the import of the conjugal act of love.

Human nature links mutual self-donation and procreation in the bodily sexual union between a man and woman. Any attempt to

---

13. Pruss, *One Body*, 263.

disengage them does not do justice to the natural greatness of spousal love. To act contrary to the procreative meaning of marital union is to undermine that union. But to engage in sexual activity only for the purpose of reproduction is to have a sexual union without an authentic personal union, without the love and sincere commitment necessary to care for children.

# Natural family planning

The necessary disposition of readiness for parenthood is not incompatible with the avoidance of having children under certain conditions. Thus, Wojtyła accepts natural family planning whereby the couple adapts themselves to the laws of nature. It is enough that a couple accepts the possibility of pregnancy even if they do not necessarily desire it. The couple may have valid reasons why they cannot have a child at a particular time, although they should still remain willing to be parents and should even regret that they cannot be parents. On the other hand, the aggressive method of contraception conflicts not only with the order of nature but with love itself, because it reduces the content of the sexual act to one of enjoyment. Outright rejection of the possibility of parenthood is an implicit rebuke of the vocation to parenthood, which is intrinsic to marriage. But the interior attitude of readiness for parenthood justifies sexual relations from a moral point of view since no anti-unitive measures are taken. It also justifies these relations in the eyes of the Creator. Responsible conjugal love is completely tethered to responsibility for procreation. Readiness or willingness for parenthood, concludes Wojtyła, "constitutes a necessary condition of love" (p. 223).

Wojtyła's striking pronouncement that willingness for parenthood is an indispensable condition of love may seem austere and even quite radical in a culture no longer alive to virtues like chastity and selfless generosity. However, it is consistent with his personalistic approach to marriage as a fusion of the personal and natural orders. Sexual intercourse assumes the true value of love and represents the "full gift" of self only when there is an interior acceptance of the possibility of parenthood. Such willingness shows that a married couple respects the natural purpose of their sexual capacities. Respect for the person requires respect for nature. When a couple dismisses or somehow suppresses their procreative capacity, they are working against their own human nature, which seeks fulfillment through reciprocal self-giving whose fruits are parenthood and family.

Positive contraception, such as the use of birth control pills, is unacceptable because the couple acts in opposition to the reproductive striving that is such an integral part of their marital union.[14] It also works against the body's positive propensity to share its goodness and generosity by creating new life. Contraception redirects the embodied person away from the procreative end of sexual activity. This conflict with nature alters the whole character of love, which is no longer imbued with a spirit of selfless generosity. Unable to share its life of goodness, the body becomes selfish and defiant as the good of the other (including parenthood and community) is no longer served by the body. This disorder constitutes a "disturbance and undermining of the love of persons," and opens the door wide for egoism and subjectivism (p. 37).[15]

When a couple withholds their procreative capacity, they no longer have a comprehensive union, a bodily gift of the entire self. The focus of sexual relations becomes sexual enjoyment, as one person becomes an object of use for another (p. 225). But an inner willingness to accept conception, which manifests itself in *full* bodily union between a man and a woman, prevents such use. This willingness helps to protect their sexual relations from devolving into a depersonalized activity based on pleasure rather than love.

## Conjugal and periodic abstinence

Without conscious acceptance of the possibility of parenthood, a married couple should refrain from sexual relations, since those relations would no longer be ordered to their proper end of procreation. In

---

14. Ibid., 326.
15. See McAleer, *Ecstatic Morality and Sexual Politics*, 115–136.

some circumstances a man and a woman cannot or should not be parents. This situation might arise if a woman becomes too sick to bear a child. In this case the only solution consonant with the personalistic norm is abstinence. However, conjugal continence is more difficult than continence outside of marriage, because a couple becomes accustomed to regular sexual relations. Under these conditions, "refraining from intercourse must encounter certain resistance and difficulties" (p. 224).

Despite the sacrifice, conjugal abstinence is the only valid course of action when procreation is ruled out. The alternative of contracepted intercourse is morally unacceptable. Given the link between the unitive and procreative dimensions of the conjugal act, when readiness for parenthood is positively excluded by contraception, "what is left (objectively speaking) in the conjugal act is sexual use alone" (p. 225). But man must live in an honorable way that demands the highest regard for the supra-utilitarian value of the person. The only honorable course of action is complete conjugal abstinence, for "whoever does not want the effect, avoids the cause" (p. 226).

In less extreme cases, however, only periodic continence is called for. This means abstaining from sexual relations only during a woman's fertile period. Periodic continence relies on the natural family planning mentality. It entails a willingness to conceive a child during the act of intercourse, even if the couple does not have an explicit desire for a child at this time. Wojtyła assumes that this is morally superior to positive contraception and sees a big difference between natural family planning and artificial contraception. The natural method defended by Wojtyła regulates conception by taking advantage of infertile periods when conception cannot occur and by practicing continence when the woman is fertile. Positive contraception, on the other hand, directly interferes with the natural process of conception by suppressing fertility or sterilizing the sexual act in some way. In the first case, infertility results from the natural operation of the laws of fertility, and the couple has done nothing to render their sexual relations sterile. But in the second case, sterility is deliberately "imposed against nature," against the order established by the Creator (p. 227).

Natural family planning respects a woman's God-given fertility cycles while artificial contraception does not. In one of his later writings as Pope, John Paul II explained that "the choice of the natural rhythms involves accepting the cycle of the person, that is the woman, and thereby accepting dialogue, reciprocal respect, shared responsibility, and self-control."[16] To be sure, the difference between natural family planning and positive contraception is subtle. They both have the same purpose: avoidance of children. But they achieve that purpose in different ways. Contraceptive intercourse actively prevents an act of intercourse from being procreative, while natural family planning relies on abstinence from sexual relations during periods of fertility. In the first case a couple acts against the good of procreation, and also uses means that prevent a total union. But this is not so with natural family planning, since one does not act contrary to nature or the procreative good. An analogy might help to clarify this distinction. There are times when the truth is delicate and should not be spoken. But there is a difference between refraining from speaking the truth and telling an outright lie, which is an action contrary to the good of truth.[17]

Of course, natural family planning should not be interpreted in a pragmatic way simply as a means to the end of avoiding pregnancy for any reason. The essence of natural family planning is reliance on periodic abstinence or the virtue of temperance motivated by love of the other. When abstinence is practiced as a virtue, marital love becomes more profound as a couple makes a sacrifice for the common good of the marriage. When the practice of periodic abstinence integrates the sexual drive with the good of marriage, marital intercourse becomes a deeper expression of the love between a husband and wife. But if abstinence is only a technique rather than a virtue, if it is experienced as temporary sexual deprivation, then abstinence is "an 'alien being' to love" (p. 228).[18]

If abstinence is a virtue it will not corrupt the necessary attitude of parental readiness. Periodic abstinence during a woman's fertility cycles should not become a *de facto* method for avoiding a family or limiting the size of a family. There must be valid reasons for refraining from

---

16. John Paul II, *Familiaris Consortio*, no. 32.

17. Joseph Boyle, "Contraception and Natural Family Planning," in *Why* Humanae Vitae *Was Right*, 407–418.

18. Grisez, *Living a Christian Life*, 687–688.

sexual relations during fertile periods. Only when these reasons are valid can the purpose of avoiding children be morally justifiable. Imagine that Frank and Marie diligently use natural family planning because they want to avoid having a big family. They want only two children so that they can pursue their expensive hobbies and purchase their dream vacation house on the ocean. These are surely inadequate reasons for refraining from reproductive sex. In their case such restraint amounts to a self-centered and irresponsible refusal to bring into existence new human persons to add to their family community.

Without some further discussion on the family there is no way to appreciate the magnitude of this problem. A family is the fulfillment of marital communion. It comes to be when a couple as a one-flesh union is blessed with the gift of new life. "Parents create the family as a complement and expansion of their love" (p. 228). To create a family is to create a community, and a community should be as large as possible for the good of all the family members. Children are educated by their parents, but they also educate each other by their extensive and supportive interactions. Of course, couples must be allowed to regulate the size of their families, but they should avoid a "minimalistic attitude" (p. 229). Some circumstances demand the sacrifice of parenthood for the family's own common good. In these cases, motivated by that common good and by "a full sense of responsibility for the procreation, support, and education of their children," periodic abstinence practiced in good faith is an acceptable solution (p. 229).

# SUMMARY

This chapter on marriage has been concerned with the issue of horizontal justice or justice to our spouses and all other human persons. Justice demands that couples take seriously their ethical commitment to exclusivity and permanence, so that they will have a secure loving relationship instead of one based on use and convenience. Given the importance of the family for the larger society, the institution of marriage assumes great significance. Every society depends on a vigorous and sincere marriage culture. When a man and a woman publicly exchange their wedding vows, they are attesting to the maturity of their love and fidelity. "Love needs this acknowledgment, without which it does not feel fully itself" (p. 203). A couple's union must be justified not only in the eyes of society, but in the eyes of God through the sacrament of Marriage.

While the institution of marriage broadly justifies sexual intercourse between a man and a woman, every sexual act within that marriage requires its own internal justification; otherwise we cannot speak of "the union of persons in love" (p. 210). Marriage is a fusion of the natural and personal orders. Through marriage a couple agrees to cooperate with the Creator in giving the gift of existence to new human persons. The conjugal act also expresses a couple's marital communion and loving cooperation as their reciprocal self-giving is fully actualized in this one-flesh union. Positive contraception impedes that one-flesh unity and thereby undermines the sexual act's unitive and personal meaning. Therefore, sexual relations call for an interior attitude of readiness for parenthood, which always acknowledges both the procreative and unitive meanings of the sexual act. Parental readiness or willingness recognizes that it is wrong to deliberately frustrate procreation because the vocation to parenthood is an essential part of the vocation to marriage. The attitude of parental readiness (versus desire) strikes the right balance between overemphasis on procreation that turns attention away from one's spouse, and the positive exclusion of procreation through contraceptive techniques. The former mindset transforms marriage into an institution of fertility, and in the latter case the two persons are no longer co-creators in fruitful love but partners in an erotic experience.

Readiness for parenthood implies the suitability of depending upon a woman's natural infertility to control family size for valid reasons. When the prospect of parenthood is unrealistic for a couple, the only alternative is conjugal abstinence. Some situations call for periodic abstinence; these should rely on natural family planning instead of contraceptive intercourse, which is contra-life. However, those who practice natural family planning should not base their decisions on "the principle of convenient life," which harms both the family community and the larger society (p. 229).[19]

---

19. Ibid., 635.

# Chapter 10

# Justice to the Creator

## *(Chapter IV: Part Two)*

In a short, private memoir about his life, an older man we'll call John ruefully looked back at his past. An accomplished writer, John had led a somber and twisted life. As a child, he had felt inferior and used his good looks to compensate for that inferiority. He married in his late twenties but was chronically unfaithful. He had several children out of wedlock and persuaded one of his female companions to abort their child. He indulged in alcohol to find his muse, but his binges only created chaos for his family. John was a gifted man but lived with intense guilt for many years. He could never find a way to liquidate that guilt until his abrupt conversion to Christianity. In his memoirs he apologized to those people whom he had "used" and exploited so callously throughout his life. He even apologized to God. "I regret that I treated God so shabbily," he wrote, "and I'm so remorseful that I could never summon the energy to show him any gratitude for the wonderful gifts he bestowed upon me."

## Natural moral order and justice to God

John's reflections on the jagged trajectory of his life suggest the theme that occupies Wojtyła in the second section of Chapter IV titled

"Vocation." He shifts attention from horizontal justice to vertical justice, the justification of our sexual activities in the eyes of God. God is a Divine Person, and this opens up the possibility of a personal relationship with him. From both the Old and New Testament we learn that God relates to man as one person to another. However, the relationship between God and man is unbalanced, since God is the Creator, who sustains us in existence, and man is the creature. Therefore God has certain expectations of us and certain "rights." The duties we owe to him in justice are the corollary of those rights.

But how can we discern our duties to the Creator? Through God's work of redemption and sanctification we know that he relates to us as one person to another, and the substance of that relationship is based on love. In this "reciprocal relation" of God and man the personalistic norm finds its "first source" (p. 232). God has repeatedly demonstrated his love for us, and we owe him love and justice in return as expressed in the personalistic norm. The more fully we come to know God and appreciate his fidelity to us, the more we are aware of what we owe to him. True religion brings this obligation into sharp focus and therefore "consists in justice . . . with respect to God" (p. 232).

Justice owed to God is based on the contingency of creation. Everything the creature is and everything it hopes to be comes gratuitously from God. Every being owes its existence to God, since we all participate in a limited way in his all-inclusive perfection of existence. God is also the source of our being. Thus, creatures are dependent on God both for their origin and for their ongoing existence as imitations of his divine essence. Since we owe our very being to God, we are not "our own." We are ultimately accountable to the Creator who has a claim on us.[1]

God, the provident Creator, has also established the whole natural order. All creatures have a certain essence or nature, a definitive design that makes them what they are. That essence derives from God, who created each creature as a manifestation of his eternal Wisdom. We can describe man's essence as a body-soul unity ordered to certain goods or

---

1. See W. Norris Clarke, S.J., *The Universe as Journey* (New York: Fordham University Press, 1988), 58–82.

created ends. These goods—such as knowledge, friendship, and marriage—perfect a person's nature and draw him out of himself and back toward God. Thanks to our human design we also have features that determine how we should live. Our curiosity, for example, leads us to pursue the good of knowledge, and our sexual differences are ordered to the good of an intimate marital communion.

From these essences proceed "all dependencies, relations, and connections between them" (p. 232). Man lives in an orderly world. His dealings with other beings are shaped by the regularity made possible by every being's essential and non-arbitrary nature. Irrational beings like animals live in conformity to this natural order by acting according to the instincts proper to their species. But the rational person is able to acknowledge this order along with its Source. The person can also discern the natural moral order, how things *ought* to be, which is implicit in the order of nature. He recognizes not only a natural inclination to knowledge but that knowledge is a good that ought to be pursued. Through recognition of the natural moral order, the person shares in God's thought and in his eternal law, which is God's plan for humanity. Our acceptance of the natural moral order represents an acquiescence to the Creator's plan, a humble submission to the order he has established. "Man is just," explains Wojtyła, "by acknowledging the order of nature and preserving it in his action" (p. 232).[2]

The opposite of this view is known as "autonomism," which maintains that the moral law has its foundation in human reason alone (p. 233). Autonomism is expressed in the moral philosophy of Immanuel Kant, for whom practical reason itself is the source of universal moral norms that deserve the will's respect. But man could only be his own legislator if he were the cause of his own existence. Prior to human law is the natural moral order, which reflects the Creator's wisdom for our flourishing and perfection.

How exactly does the human person fit into this scheme? The person belongs to the natural order because he is made with a certain

2. David Oderberg, "The Metaphysical Foundations of Natural Law," in *Natural Moral Law in Contemporary Society*, ed. H. Zaborowski (Washington, D.C.: Catholic University of America Press, 2010), 76–98.

essence or human nature ordered to its own final end. But the person is not submerged in nature like other creatures. Thanks to the soul, the person can transcend nature in some ways through his ability to will, to know, and to love. Justice toward the Creator, therefore, includes two elements: submission to the order of nature and emphasis on the value of the person. The extraordinary value of the person becomes evident through his or her participation in the thought of the Creator, which allows for the "correct relation" to reality (p. 233). Through the light of human reason we are sharers in God's eternal law reflected in the natural moral order. We recognize the natural goodness and value of things, which allows us to determine the appropriate relation to them. Through this same sharing in God's wisdom it is possible to discern the correct disposition to other people, which is love as stipulated in the personalistic norm. Justice to God is impossible without love that preserves and promotes the personal order. God has created the human person, who "reflects his [God's] essence" through his spirituality and self-possession (p. 234). Hence God is the summit and source of that personal order. The just man respects the personal order through his loving-kindness of other persons, and he manifests respect for the natural order and natural ends of created reality.

In the order of nature the meaning of a human being's sexual capacities is the transmission of new life in accordance with one's human structure and sexual design. But since that human being is also a person, we cannot compare married, conjugal life to the sexual life of animals. Sexual relations must always be elevated to the level of love so that they assume a personal character. In this way, sexual relations constitute a communion between two persons, who in their reciprocal self-giving bring about new human life. Justice to God, therefore, demands respect for the purpose of the sexual drive along with the structure of our sexual design, including the complementarity of male and female. That complementarity makes possible this sexual union, which can transmit new life. It is precisely for this reason that conjugal relations "must be permeated with a readiness for parenthood" (p. 235). But justice to God also requires acknowledging that sexual union is an expression of an exclusive interpersonal union and total sharing indicative of spousal love. As we saw in Chapter Nine, the natural and personal orders are interdependent. If we sincerely want to be just to the Creator, we cannot act contrary to nature, because by doing so we act contrary to the good of the person.

## The meaning of virginity

In this context, then, justice to God implies respect for the complexity of marriage, recognizing God's supreme but reasonable rights "in the sphere of nature and in the sphere of the person" (p. 235). It would seem, however, that the rights of the Creator over his creatures are both extensive and demanding. Each being owes his existence to the Creator, and the act of existence is the root of all the "perfections of a given being" (p. 235). Each person is "completely a possession of the Creator" (p. 235). Comprehensive justice, therefore, seems to demand that I go farther than adherence to the personalistic norm; that I offer to God all that is in me, my whole being. According to Aquinas, justice is the secure willingness to give others what is theirs or what is owed to them.[3] But we can never be just to God because we can never give what is due to him. Even a total giving of oneself to God cannot balance the "scales of justice" and somehow "repay" him for the gift of existence and the perfections that flow from that existence.

Thus, a relationship with God centered on justice alone is impossible. Man's relationship to God must be based primarily on love, rather than on the repayment of a debt or rendering to God what is owed to him. Christ has shown that self-giving has its foundation in such love, for love "facilitates a way from one person to another, from man to God" (p. 236). Love also raises man's relationship with God to a higher level, since love (but not justice) aims at the unification of persons through reciprocal self-giving.

When we understand our relationship with God in this way, the total self-gift associated with virginity acquires its full meaning. Virginity means "intactness" that comes from a life of sexual abstinence. In marriage, a person gives his or her whole body to another and loses this intactness. A person can choose to give himself totally to God

---

3. Saint Thomas Aquinas, *Summa Theologiae* II–II, q. 58, a, 1c.

rather than enter into conjugal relations emblematic of reciprocal self-giving. The total and exclusive gift of self to the Creator is the essence of spiritual virginity, which is "spousal love directed to God himself" (p. 237). Spiritual virginity suggests physical virginity or "intactness," the abstention from marriage and sexual intercourse. The person who chooses to give himself or herself to God links this gift with his or her physical virginity. Virginity, therefore, comes to signify that the whole person, body and soul, belongs exclusively to God, for what was a natural condition now becomes an object of will and deliberate choice. Virginity is connected with intactness, but intactness does not necessarily imply virginity. Virginity is giving oneself to God, and one effect of that gift is the preclusion of sexual intercourse. Wojtyła explains that "the person choosing the total and exclusive self-giving to God binds it with intactness, which he decides to preserve" (p. 237).

The essential meaning of virginity is not to be found in the relinquishing of marriage but in the need to give oneself to another. This need to give oneself goes beyond the sexual drive; it has deeply rooted origins that are connected with the existence and spiritual nature of each human person. As we observed in Chapter Four, all being has an innate generosity by which it communicates its presence and shares its goodness with others. All being as an act of existence is a dynamism toward self-communication. At the personal level this takes the form of love, of going out toward others by sharing one's gifts and inner resources. Thus, the need to give oneself is latent in every person who perfects his nature through self-giving (and receiving).[4]

How does a person fulfill this interior dynamism, this "need to give himself to another person" (p. 239)? Most people choose marriage as a way to live out the vocation of spousal love, but some generously choose the path of virginity and consecration to God. Virginity is a perfect path to spousal love for those who do not marry. It represents a movement toward "final union with the personal God through love" (p. 240). In his praise for the value of virginity, Wojtyła is careful not to belittle marriage in any way. Virginity does not presuppose the

---

4. W. Norris Clarke, S.J., *Person and Being* (Milwaukee: Marquette University Press, 1993), 75–76.

superiority of spiritual to bodily or sexual values. That viewpoint is more typical of the philosophy of Manichaeanism, which regards the body as alien and inferior to the spiritual soul. Marriage is not just about bodily union but also involves the realm of the spirit. Marital communion represents the giving of one's whole self, body and soul, to one's spouse. Marriage typically is easier for most men and women, and therefore virginity is "something exceptional" (p. 240). The real value of virginity does not lie in intactness or abstinence from sexual relations. Nor does it suggest the primacy of the spirit over body and matter. Virginity is to be greatly esteemed for its role in realizing the kingdom of God on earth. The virgin's exclusive self-donation and "belonging" to God anticipates our eternal union with God and points us toward our universal destiny.

## The meaning of vocation

This discussion of marriage and consecrated life in *Love and Responsibility* shifts to a concise treatment of the related theme of vocation. A vocation is not found in the world of things or animals, where there is no possibility of conscious self-determination. A chipmunk does not have a vocation but merely lives according to its instincts. Vocation is peculiar to the human person, because only a rational being can make a personal commitment to a particular purpose. Only a person can consciously and freely envision an end (such as becoming a doctor) and pursue the necessary means to achieve that end over an extended period of time.

All human persons have a vocation, an interior calling that illuminates a proper course of development to follow. Vocation, however, does not simply mean a career choice or a calling to some profession, but has a far deeper meaning. It implies a commitment of one's whole life in the service of certain values. Every person must discern this direction by recognizing his gifts and inner resources that enable him to serve others in some way. At its most fundamental level, having a vocation means loving someone and being prepared to give oneself for love. Every person has the natural vocation to give himself or herself to others. Such self-giving has a profound creative effect because it generates loving relationships through which the person can find himself or herself and achieve fulfillment (p. 242).

Both virginity and marriage are vocations, since they are proper responses to the human vocation to love, a calling that wells up from the depth of one's being. However, if marriage is regarded as a purely materialistic arrangement for convenience or mutual sexual satisfaction, then it is not a true vocation. The basis for a valid vocation must always fall within the "personalistic vision of human existence," where there is a conscious and free desire both to share one's inner resources of wisdom and love and to care about the good of the other (p. 243). The question, "What is my vocation?" has a simple but profound meaning: "In which direction should the development of my personhood proceed in light of what I have in myself, what I can give of myself, what others— people and God—expect from me?" (p. 243).

The interior life of the person, however, which moves us in the direction of this generosity and spousal love, is not the sole source of one's calling. An objective call from God accompanies the inner need we have to determine the direction of our development by love. In the New Testament we learn that everyone has the same vocation or calling to self-perfection through love. This calling can be lived out in many different ways, such as married life or consecrated virginity. But we cannot achieve such self-perfection by simply relying on our own resources. Hence the Gospel also requires us to believe in divine grace and to rely on God's help. God's abundant graces insert man into the "orbit of the action of God," where we receive his love. The mature solution to any vocational dilemma is how we respond to that love. Thus the call to love is the primary vocation of every person, for above all we must strive to fulfill the commandment to love God and our neighbor. A person's state in life plays only a "secondary role" (p. 244).

## Vocation to parenthood

In the context of this broad discussion on vocation, Wojtyła reflects on the vocation of parenthood, which is an essential part of the vocation to marriage. Parenthood, however, should not be seen merely in terms of biological parenthood that results from bringing a child into the world. Considered on a personal level, parenthood both crystallizes and confirms the love between a man and a woman and perfects the marital union. Parenthood is not an extraordinary or "irregular" state, because it has deep roots within a man and woman who long for a child to complete their union. This is especially true for a woman, whose whole organism is designed for the sake of motherhood and the nurturing of her newborn child.

By giving life to a baby, a man and woman reaffirm their own intrinsic value and fruitful goodness. All being is good, and the nature of the good is to express and give itself. Nowhere is this innate fecundity more evident than in the giving of human life. A husband and wife not only give physical life through their intimate union, but they also help endow that child's life with spiritual maturity by forming its inner self. "For the person is, in a sense, more 'interiority' than a 'body'" (p. 245). Fatherhood and motherhood, therefore, are not limited to biology and the transmission of new life but reach much deeper. They represent a form of "spiritual perfection," which consists in some generation in a spiritual sense. Thus, physical parenthood must be supplemented and supported by spiritual parenthood through education and moral formation.

All human persons, not just biological parents, possess the vocation to spiritual parenthood. Spiritual motherhood or fatherhood is a distinct characteristic of a "mature interior personhood" (p. 246). Spiritual maternity or paternity also shows how men and women naturally seek to go out toward others, to share their innate goodness, particularly their wisdom and love. This dynamic desire to share the gifts to be found in one's interior spiritual treasury is especially directed to young children, who gladly seize the opportunity to learn. And the love that develops for spiritual fathers and mothers closely resembles the love parents have for their children. Spiritual kinship, which is based on the bonds between souls, is "often stronger than the kinship that results from the bonds of blood alone" (p. 246).

Spiritual parenthood is a worthy goal for all human beings that is consistent with the Gospel call to constantly strive for perfection through self-giving love. We must remember that God the Father is the supreme model of that perfection. When we give of ourselves as spiritual parents, our actions resemble the self-communicative love of the Trinity. Hence a person, elevated by grace, will attain a likeness to God the Creator when this spiritual parenthood, "whose archetype is God, is also formed in him" (p. 246). By giving himself generously in this spiritual way a person perfects himself and becomes an image of divine perfection. Spiritual parenthood brings us beyond the world of nature, where a child has only two biological parents, into the world of persons, where many people can cooperate in the development of the child. Any attempt to denigrate this broad and multi-faceted vocation to parenthood "is contrary to the natural paths of man's development" (p. 247).

## Summary

We might conclude this chapter by briefly reviewing what is to be gained by framing the issues of sexual morality in terms of justice to the Creator.

First, we are reminded that in all areas of morality we are not completely autonomous, and we do not create our own moral laws. This is because our human nature or structure is given to us, and that nature expresses goods and values. God is the origin of the natural order, which includes the natural moral order. This natural law, which is initially promulgated through the design of our human nature, is a manifestation of the eternal law, God's providential plan for his creatures. All our actions must be in harmony with the natural moral order if we are to be just in our dealings with God.

Second, men and women called to pursue the vocation of marriage must acknowledge that marriage is a fusion of the natural and personal orders, which have their origin in God. Hence the attitude of readiness for parenthood is not necessary only for the justification of the sexual act from the perspective of the personalistic norm which forbids use of another. It also shows proper deference to God's provident plan for sexual differentiation ordered to a complementary and fruitful union.

Third, the only way we can begin to repay God for his many gifts is to live out our innate vocation to love God sincerely along with our neighbor. All persons have a natural inclination for spousal love, which comes to light in our lives as the law of the gift, "inscribed deeply in the very being of the person" (p. 285). This form of reciprocal self-giving can be realized through marriage and also through virginity, which is spousal love directed to God himself. With the help of God's graces, every person must strive to freely share his or her inner resources and gifts with others. To be a person is to love. To love is to expand oneself with the help of the beloved and to become more like the God who made us.[5]

---

5. Ibid., 81–84.

# Chapter 11

# Concluding Thoughts

In an essay he wrote in 1965, Wojtyła explained that we shouldn't think of sexual morality in purely naturalistic terms that exclude personalistic categories.[1] *Love and Responsibility*, of course, represents Wojtyła's effort to rethink sexual morality from a personalist perspective. In his mind, it is preferable to construct a sexual ethic by focusing primarily on the incomparable dignity of the human person in judging which forms of sexual behavior are either morally permissible or forbidden. The personalistic norm, which must be conditioned by the natural moral order, becomes the measure of behavior in the sexual sphere. Thus, positive contraception is wrong not just because if its disharmony with nature, but also because it undermines the marital communion a couple seeks through their embodied personhood. Without that full union of mind, heart, and body, and without a willingness for children who perfect that union, the door is open for mutual pleasure-seeking that depersonalizes the marital relationship.

---

1. Karol Wojtyła, "The Problem of Catholic Sexual Ethics," in *Person and Community*, 284.

Wojtyła's whole philosophical enterprise aims at a theory of sexual morality that does justice to the person. It also takes carefully into account the natural order—our sexual complementarity designed by the Creator along with the natural purpose of our sexual capacities. The reader will have to judge how well Wojtyła has succeeded in his ambitious project. Are his arguments convincing enough to persuade a new generation of vulnerable Catholics that the sexual revolution's hedonistic ideology and narcissism degrade the human person? Can our natural reasoning powers give us access to a moral truth that complements New Testament teachings on sexual morality, so that we can better understand those teachings and live them more freely?

This final chapter offers a brief summary of Wojtyła's work in the hope of revealing its underlying cogency. We climb to higher ground so that the reader can appreciate the logical flow of Wojtyła's overarching argument. This summary is presented in fairly bold strokes in order to grasp the skeletal structure and moral logic of such a difficult treatise. Along the way I will offer a modest defense of Wojtyła's primary arguments and try to highlight their internal consistency. The aim is to demonstrate that Wojtyła's personalistic approach to sexual morality can easily withstand the scrutiny of his critics.

## Summary points

If we sift through the vast material in *Love and Responsibility*, we can identify the key steps in Wojtyła's overall argument that can serve as a summary:

❈ By nature all human beings are equal. Each one of them has a natural dignity by virtue of his or her rational soul. This rational soul (or reason) allows a human being to be a person with an inner life that revolves around truth and goodness.[2] Reason "constitutes the basis of personhood" and conditions the person's

---

2. As Wojtyła explained in one of his essays, "every person has a rational nature because of a spiritual soul, which is the substantial form of the body" (*Person and Community*, 168).

"'inwardness' and spirituality" (p. 207). Thanks to reason, every person possesses himself. This simply means that he is aware of himself and can freely determine his own destiny through choices made by the will collaborating with reason. Each person is unique and incommunicable, an independent being with his or her own goals, hopes, and aspirations. The human person is an "embodied spirit," a natural unity of a masculine or feminine body and a rational soul. Otherwise we end up with a dualistic view of the person as two discrete substances (spirit and matter). That view cannot be easily defended. Finally, every person is a social being with the innate capability of giving himself, and this law of the gift is "indispensable *for the union of persons*" (p. 286). Wojtyła's conception of personhood is the fertile but stable ground for his entire ethical system.

❊ Above all, that moral system must measure up to the dignity and excellence of the human person, who exists for herself and to give herself to others. In our interactions with all human persons, we can treat them in two broad possible ways: we can either love the person by respecting his or her morally reasonable self-chosen ends, *or* we can use the person merely as an instrument to achieve our own self-serving needs. Using another person cannot be justified, since it depersonalizes and does violence to that person. Rather, each person must be loved and affirmed for his or her own sake. Wojtyła calls this supreme moral principle the *personalistic norm*. That norm has a bi-dimensional content: "the positive ('love') and the negative ('do not use')" (p. 156).

❊ The personalistic principle is warranted because if we disavow it, we must concede that it is morally acceptable to manipulate other persons rather than treat them with loving-kindness. This leads to inconsistency, for no rational or healthy individual likes to be used or selfishly manipulated by someone else. The rival ethical theory of utilitarianism, however, argues that right actions are those that maximize happiness, which is defined as the overall balance of pleasure over pain. Utilitarianism fails because it inevitably persuades us to regard other persons as a *means* to bring about happiness (or pleasure). Persons can be used for this end in two ways: ordinary manipulation, and for pleasure or sexual enjoyment. In the latter case one isolates pleasure in the sexual act and treats it as a distinct aim of activity. The personalistic norm and utilitarianism represent two fundamentally different moral visions, but only the former is compatible with the Gospel.

❀ Addressing the issue of sexual pleasure and its proper role in the cultivation of romantic love is central to any cogent treatment of sexual morality. The second and related issue concerns our sexual design and the purpose of our sexual capacities. Questions of sexual morality are delicate, because we must differentiate romantic love from the intention to "use" a person even when use "keeps the appearance of love and uses love's name as its own" (p. 18). Sex motivated solely by the agreeable sensation of pleasure cannot stand up to the personalistic norm because pleasure is so subjective. It is not an objective good that provides fulfillment. A person does not show his love and respect for someone through the pursuit of mutual pleasure sanctioned by utilitarianism. Our fulfillment as persons is to be found in objective goods such as health and knowledge that truly enhance our well-being and not in the satisfaction of sexual desires we happen to have.

❀ We might take pleasure in using our sexual capacities, but pleasure is not their purpose. In order to explain that purpose, Wojtyła discusses the sexual drive, which is a natural drive in all human beings that directs us to a person of the opposite sex. The sexual drive has its foundation in sexual difference, which directs a man and a woman to each other and opens the way for a deep personal union. In this union, two incomplete and complementary parts form a natural, unified whole ordered to the biological end of reproduction. Wojtyła describes the sexual drive as a "certain orientation" that must be perfected and given shape by acts of will at the level of the person (p. 30). The human species can only be sustained if individuals follow the sexual drive, although they should only do so when that drive develops into love. Sexuality has a procreative meaning because our sexual capacities exist for the purpose of perpetuating the human species. The sexual drive also has an *existential meaning*, because when a man and a woman come together in sexual union, they can bring a new human person into existence, and existence is the root of all other perfections. Personal being is the highest form of existence, and this accounts for the "proper greatness of this drive" (p. 35). Thus, the final cause or natural purpose of sexual activity is procreation. Because the sacred new life that results from procreative activity is best nurtured in stable families, procreation should be confined to marriage.

❀ It follows from the purpose and existential meaning of the sexual drive that the "common good" of marriage is procreation and the raising of children. Other ends include sharing a life together (marital unity or friendship) and the proper enjoyment of sexual intimacy. These marital goods can only be realized as a single complex aim since the unitive and procreative meanings of marriage are closely intertwined. Like other moralists, Wojtyła appreciates that marriage is a complex but unified good such that its unitive goodness is inseparable from its procreative goodness.[3] A man and a woman can avoid using each other in sexual relations only when they pursue the common good of marriage rather than focus on satisfying their own sexual impulses.

❀ After clarifying nature's purpose for our sexual powers, Wojtyła turns to the second major issue of sexual morality: how to differentiate love from errant sexual desire and pleasure-seeking, which are responsible for the "distortions" that can occur in love between a man and a woman (p. 27). In order to understand the nature of love he analyzes it under three aspects: the metaphysics of love, the psychology of love, and the ethics of love. If people are to be loved and not used, we must come to a thorough understanding

---

3. John Finnis, "The Good of Marriage and the Morality of Sexual Relations," *American Journal of Jurisprudence* 42 (1997), 125.

of love, especially spousal love. The metaphysical analysis considers love's general characteristics. These include fondness, love of desire or longing for the other as a good to be possessed, and benevolence. Benevolence represents a caring for the other's good, an "altruistic turning" of the will toward the other's well-being (p. 66). Benevolence puts us in close proximity to the essence of love. Love also includes reciprocity based on altruism, sympathy (or affective love), and friendship. Friendship represents an ongoing or "full" commitment to the other, a moral unity that can even be called "a doubling of the 'I'" (p. 74).

❈ Love has many forms, but the "fullest" form of human love is spousal love between two persons. Spousal love means "giving oneself," and "'to give oneself' means more than merely 'to want the good'" for another (p. 78). Spousal love is characterized by exclusivity and mutual self-donation or self-surrender. Unlike animals, the conscious person with free will can rise above the limitations of matter and choose to totally devote herself to another. Paradoxically, through this total self-donation the person is not diminished but enriched and expanded. The most common form of spousal love is lived out in the vocation of marriage. This exclusive and unconditional gift of self is consummated in the fruitful sexual act, which uniquely expresses spousal love. Sexual intercourse reflects the reality that spousal love "is not only a spiritual union of persons, but also a bodily . . . one" (p. 196). Sexual relations retain their unifying power only as an "expression of this mature union" (p. 109).

❈ The psychological analysis focuses on the catalysts for love that "happen" in our body and psyche to help create the psychological state of love. Love between a man and a woman has both physical and emotional components, which Wojtyła calls sensuality and affectivity respectively. Sensuality is an experience of the sexual values associated with the body of a person of the opposite sex. Affectivity is an experience of the sexual values linked with the whole person, such as a woman's feminine charm and gentle demeanor or a man's virility. These two forces constitute the "raw material" for romantic attraction that can grow into spousal love. Sensuality and affectivity create the conditions for love, but they are not love itself. However, many people mistake love for sensual attraction and amorous sentiment. For real love to blossom, these sensual and affective experiences must be integrated with the nobler aspects of love such as friendship and benevolence. The beloved is then seen not merely as an attractive body, but as a person, as *someone* to be cared for and affirmed for his or her own sake.

❀ The need for this integration suggests the ethical character of love, the third part of Wojtyła's analysis of love between a man and a woman. Four requirements are necessary for spousal love to be lived out as a virtue, as something far superior to a relationship based on sensuality and affectivity. First, spousal love must be "permeated" with an affirmation of the value of the person or it will become a disintegrated love (p. 105); it is especially important for a couple to give priority to the value of the person over sexual values. Second, the essence of spousal love is reciprocal self-giving, which creates a belonging to each other in an exclusive and permanent relationship whose expression is sexual intercourse. But sexual union without that reciprocal belonging and interpersonal union loses its integrity and unifying power. Third, spousal love means assuming responsibility for the beloved's well-being and fulfillment. Persons must be suitable for each other so that they can truly belong to one another, and find themselves in their spouse. The importance of compatibility underscores the need to be extremely conscientious in the choice of a spouse. Finally, love depends on freedom, and the "authentic commitment of freedom" depends on truth (p. 117). My free commitment to another person must be based on the truth about that person, so the will is unencumbered by illusion or erratic emotions that distort the truth. Self-giving is deprived of its virtuous character if it is based on compulsion or irrational attachment. Spousal love is always a free striving for interpersonal union and the other's good in a way that takes the lover far beyond herself in the quest for that good.

❀ Thanks to the power of sensuality, authentic spousal love is threatened by concupiscence, a tendency to covet the other person merely as a possible object of enjoyment. So the virtue of love requires the companion virtue of chastity, which protects love's true character. Chastity guards love from the sensual and emotional reactions that can undermine the transparency needed for the free gift of self. Concupiscence, the result of our fallen sexuality, can lead to sinful love if it slides from interest in another's sexual values into desire and then cascades into "willing" or actively seeking to use another as an object for pleasure. Affectivity, which is focused on sexual values associated with the whole person, may seem like an antidote for concupiscence. But in reality affectivity does little to protect the self from concupiscence, "the hotbed of sin." Moreover, affectivity often evolves into "emotional subjectivism," with the person fully self-absorbed in his feelings. This state can progress into a subjectivism of values that elevates pleasure—whatever feels good—to the highest level in the hierarchy of values. Subjectivism, which suggests that internal feelings and moods are all that really matter, is the ground of egoism. It is a small step from egoism, where the self is fixated on its own good "in an exclusive, narrow way," to sinful love, in which affection or sensual pleasure takes precedence over the value of the person (p. 139). In sinful love based on sensuality, the person is abstracted from the body, which becomes an object of consumption.

❀ One can only combat concupiscence through chastity. This virtue is more than simply temperance or the moderation of sexual desire. Chastity in its full sense means the liberation of love from the pernicious attitudes that bring about using others for pleasure. Chastity is a "'transparency' of interiority," a disposition to see the other always as a person through the fog of sensual and emotional attraction (p. 154). Chastity enables us to recognize the body not as the ground of appropriation or an object of use, but as a means of creating communion through the sincere gift of self. The essence of chastity, therefore, consists in a habitual readiness to affirm the value of the person in every situation. Chastity does not imply the repudiation of sexual values but their integration with the value of the person. Chastity also makes possible a clearer knowledge of the other person's spiritual and moral traits. This knowledge opens the way for a free commitment and a truly *personal union*. Only the chaste man and the chaste woman are capable of love, because chastity liberates their relationship from any inclination to use the other.

❀ The two components of chastity are shame and abstinence. Wojtyła describes sexual shame as a defense mechanism against those who would seek to use a person as a sexual object. A woman dresses modestly to counteract the concupiscent look of men, while the chaste man seeks to subdue his more aggressive sexual nature. Shame "charts the direction of all sexual morality" because it preserves our ability to affirm the value of the person in the face of concupiscence (p. 162). The experience of shame reflects the essential nature of the person, who belongs to herself and who resists being objectified and virtually "possessed" by someone else. The second ingredient of chastity is abstinence, for the chaste person is always the self-possessed person. Thanks to his self-mastery in the sexual realm, the chaste man finds the proper amount of sensual excitability and affective sensibility. When necessary, self-mastery is accomplished through abstinence, but blind abstinence does not rise to the level of virtue. Abstinence becomes a virtue only when it is done for the sake of the value of the person. When the person "takes the lead" in our conscious experiences, there is an opening for giving ourselves to others through self-transcending love (p. 182).

❀ In the face of concupiscence, spousal love depends on chastity, since love always demands an affirmation of the value of the person. Spousal love also needs the support of a sincere marriage culture. There must be an "appropriate framework" to help foster and protect this love, and that framework is marriage (p. 195). It is only in marriage that the purpose of the sexual urge can be properly acknowledged and honored, and the personalistic norm duly respected. Marriage is defined by the features of indissolubility and monogamy, which follow from that norm. A declaration of love implies "forever" and contradicts itself when it is qualified by temporal limits. Moreover, marriage is indissoluble because if love is based on the *objective value* of the other person, it cannot wither away or be withdrawn. A retraction of spousal love objectifies the other who is "disposed of" or victimized by insincere spousal commitment. Man and woman become one flesh and cannot separate without causing great damage to themselves and others. Polygamy is immoral because it strikes at the heart of the total union and exclusivity essential to marriage. Monogamy follows from the nature of spousal love itself. When a person gives himself or herself totally in marriage, this act "excludes . . . the simultaneous self-giving on his or her part to other persons in the same way" (p. 82).

❀ Marriage is a social institution because every society has a vested interest in the family or the "small society," which is the foundation for larger societies (p. 201). The public exchange of wedding vows signals a couple's mature sexual relationship based on a love that "durably joins and unifies them" (p. 204). Sexual relations must also be justified in the eyes of God as well as in the eyes of civil society. This justification occurs through the sacrament of Marriage. In addition, every conjugal act must possess its own "interior justice" so that sexual union always expresses a total union and sharing between these two married persons (p. 210). A married couple has a vocation to parenthood because they enter the natural order and choose to participate in creation. But marriage is not just about reproduction. Rather, marriage represents the fusion of the order of nature and the personal order. Authentic conjugal love, therefore, cannot bypass the link between total personal bodily union and procreation. Marriage has a unitive meaning as spouses engage in the sexual act for the purpose of giving themselves, body and soul, to each other exclusively and completely. The sexual act also has a procreative meaning since this comprehensive bodily union is naturally oriented toward procreation. Positive contraception always impedes this one-flesh unity of man and woman. As a result, sexual relations within marriage have their full value as a union of persons only when the spouses consciously accept parenthood and family, which represent important goods for each of them. When both persons in a marital union act "in conformity with the interior logic of love," they are prepared to accept the fruitful gift of new life as an "expression of the creative power of love" (p. 216). This attitude of readiness for parenthood captures the right balance between overemphasis on procreation and its positive exclusion. Parental readiness is consistent with natural family planning and periodic abstinence under appropriate conditions.

❈ In addition to horizontal justice in our relationships with others, there must also be vertical justice, or justice to the Creator. God is a Personal Being to whom we owe all gifts, especially the gift of our existence. Since human persons owe their existence to God, they are not merely "their own," and must be accountable to him. Justice to the Creator demands respect for the natural order and the natural laws that reflect the Creator's wisdom for human flourishing. It also implies respect for the value of the person, who reflects God's essence in her ability to love. For a married couple, justice to the Creator is realized by respecting the good of marriage. That good includes a couple's vocation to parenthood as well as a sharing together of their lives in an exclusive cooperative relationship, where each member of this couple finds himself or herself through spousal love.

❈ However, a relationship with God based on justice is untenable, since it is impossible to give God his due, what is owed to him. That relationship must be based on love. Some persons choose to devote their lives to God and to develop an intimate relationship with him that shapes their whole life. They choose a life of spiritual virginity, which is "spousal love directed to God himself" (p. 237). Spiritual virginity is often accompanied by sexual "intactness" or purity that symbolizes their exclusive belonging to God rather than to a spouse. All persons have a vocation to spousal love inscribed into their being. Most choose marriage to live out their vocation, but some choose virginity as a way of fulfilling this interior dynamism to give one's self to another.

This extensive summary shows that after laying the necessary groundwork, Wojtyła deals with five principal themes: the perfection of the person through love, the nature of spousal love, the existential character of the sexual drive, chastity, and marriage. Persons are created to love and to be loved, for "the person finds in love the greatest fullness of his being" (p. 66). The most basic form of love represents affirming the person for his or her own sake and not interfering with a person's pursuit of her own fulfillment. As we have seen, Wojtyła refers to this principle as the personalistic norm. Each person thrives when he is loved and affirmed by others. But a person's life is also enriched and expanded when he gives himself, communicating his own inner gifts and riches to others. This dynamic of self-giving and receiving "perfects the being of the person and develops his existence" (p. 66).

All love aims at union and binding commitment along with the good of the beloved. Spousal love is a reciprocal self-giving of persons that creates a deeper interpersonal connection than other forms of love. A person can give himself either to a human person or to God. Spousal love, the fullest and "most radical form of love," exemplifies the "perfecting of oneself . . . through love" (p. 80). Loving another involves "transcending one's 'I'" and getting beyond one's limits and selfish interests (p. 78). Spousal love represents the deepest form of self-transcendence, not just willing the other's good but reaching out in self-oblivious love to give one's whole self to another person. Friendship and other types of love "do not reach as far as spousal love" (p. 78). In this radical act, the person discovers himself, for "whoever loses his life . . . will find it" (Mt 16:25). Spousal love, therefore, unveils the path to genuine human fulfillment and mature self-possession. "Through the gift of self," explains Wojtyła, the person "deepens the self-possession and self-governance proper to himself" (p. 283).

For a man and a woman, spousal love creates a fully committed interpersonal and bodily union that is expressed through sexual relations. In spousal love, the sexual drive realizes its procreative potential, because "the proper end of the drive . . . is the existence of the species *Homo sapiens*" (p. 35). Hence the existential character of the sexual drive.

The primary purpose of sexual relations, therefore, is procreation, while the secondary purpose is strengthening the bonds of conjugal union. A sexual union without the altruistic spirit and unconditional commitment of spousal love is not a loving, *personal* union. In a truly loving union, two people give their total embodied selves (including their fertility) to each other. Thereby they become fulfilled through this mutual self-donation, which comes to ultimate fruition in the form of new life. Positive contraception defies the sexual drive's natural "bond" with existence. It also interferes with this reciprocal self-giving and fails to affirm the full value of the other as an embodied person. Within such a personal union of total sharing, the goods of parenthood and family cannot be positively excluded by acting contrary to nature without the rejection of the maternal or paternal *personhood* of the other.[4]

Untamed concupiscence, subjectivism, and egoism are the implacable foes of love. They stand in the way of forming a personal union. But the virtue of chastity emancipates us from these forces deep within the self that foster a utilitarian attitude, which is the antithesis of love. Chastity clarifies our vision and makes love possible by allowing us to always affirm "the value of the person in every situation" (p. 155). Chastity also prevents the isolation of the person from the body, whereby the other is desired as an object of gratification rather than as a person to be loved. Spousal love's "kinship" with chastity allows for its proper growth and development.

Spousal love also needs the institutional and sacramental support of marriage. Within marriage a couple live out their conjugal covenant, which includes the vocation to parenthood. Marriage is a community of persons with a husband and wife at its nucleus who form an indissoluble bond. They affirm each other for their own sake and care for each other. Their personal union is expressed in a sexual union whereby the two become one flesh, and it is fulfilled through the fruitful gift of new life. That personal union of total sharing is good in itself, and is fortified when the family grows.[5]

---

4. Crosby, "Wojtyła's Personalist Understanding of Man and Woman," 261.

5. Patrick Lee, "Marriage, Procreation, and Same-Sex Unions," *The Monist*, vol. 91, no. 3 (2008), 427–435.

In marriage, which proceeds from the "interiority" or inner nature of spousal love, two persons commit to totally give themselves to each other and strive for the other's good (p. 293). They generously welcome children (within their means) and provide those new *persons* with an intimate community where they can flourish by giving and receiving love. Only marriage can ensure that the dignity of all persons involved in these relationships will be properly respected. Thus, we see that the principal themes of *Love and Responsibility* fit together like interlocking parts to reveal a coherent theory of sexual morality centered on the incomparable value of the person.

## The metaphysical basis of Wojtyła's argument

Wojtyła's analysis of love has a strong foundation. It is grounded in a holistic metaphysical vision that is focused on the metaphysics of the good and the human person's place within the natural order of being. Wojtyła's frequent references to the objective order of nature affirm his commitment to a Thomistic vision of the created universe. That universe consists of *real beings* with an act of existence, limited by a finite essence that defines what they are. Wojtyła implicitly follows the philosophy of Aquinas as he integrates his description of the experience of love with these key metaphysical premises.[6]

Recall Wojtyła's discussion of the existential meaning of the sexual drive, for it is through the sexual drive that a new human person comes into existence. Existence is not simply a fact or state of affairs but the "first and fundamental good," the central core of all other perfections (p. 35). "Existence," explains Wojtyła, "determines all that the given being is and what it has in itself" (p. 235). According to Aquinas, all being is an *act* of existence or presence, so that *to be* always means to be actually present to others. Because of this inner energy, every being is a natural dynamism that wants to communicate or express itself, and thereby share its own goodness with others. As Aquinas explains, "It is

---

6. Clarke, S.J., *The Creative Retrieval of St. Thomas Aquinas*, 89–94.

in the nature of every actuality to communicate itself insofar as it is possible."[7]

In the person this act of presence becomes enlightened self-presence so that the person possesses himself through self-awareness and self-determination. The fullness of being, therefore, is personal being or self-possessing presence. The person "transcends the world of nature" and exists more intensely because he is not completely submerged in matter (p. 234). For Aquinas, "the person is that which is the most perfect in all of nature."[8] At the personal level, conscious, free, self-expressive action takes the form of love and self-donation. As Wojtyła explains, we find "inscribed in the nature of the personal being the potency and power of giving oneself" (p. 281).

Given this metaphysical perspective, it is logical for Wojtyła to deduce an "organic link of ethics with metaphysics" (p. 284). He suggests that metaphysics confirms his conclusions about sexual ethics and spousal love. Our aspirations for spousal love are not accidental or culturally conditioned, but rooted in the very nature of our being. It is the nature of every person to go out of himself toward others in love, sharing his or her gifts for the sake of the other's good. Of course, no one can give himself unless he transcends himself, and the model of personal being as self-transcending is spousal love. Wojtyła refers to this dynamism as "'the law of the gift,' which is written not merely in the body alone and its sexual distinctness, but in the very person" (p. 288). Such love and self-giving builds intimate community, an interpersonal sharing and receiving, which is most fully expressed among human persons in spousal (or marital) love. This love can be authentic only when it is charitably open to new life and exhibits the full self-transcendence and generosity proper to the procreative act. In spousal love, the person reflects at the deepest level the innate generosity of being itself. In this form of love, created being, which is an image of the Creator, reaches the height of generosity. The fruit of that

---

7. Saint Thomas Aquinas, *De Potentia*, q. 2, art. 1. See also Clarke, S.J., *Explorations in Metaphysics*, 45–64.

8. Saint Thomas Aquinas, *Summa Theologiae*, q. 29, art. 3. See also Clarke, *Explorations in Metaphysics*, 15–16.

generosity is the gift of new life, the "natural perfection" of being (p. 245). When we follow this "law of the gift," therefore, we perfect our being through love as we create a communion of persons that leads to our authentic fulfillment.[9]

## Defending Wojtyła's anthropology

What about the validity of Wojtyła's analysis? His sexual ethic may be perfectly consistent with New Testament teachings and Catholic doctrine, but do its underlying philosophical arguments have merit? Has he in fact succeeded in explaining these norms with sufficient clarity and in convincing us that they are justified in the light of natural reason? A full evaluation is beyond the scope of this book, so we must be content with defending the primary theses of his presentation and pointing out a few of its specific moral implications.

Wojtyła believed that an erroneous anthropology or understanding of the human person would impede a proper treatment of ethics. The anthropological premises underlying Wojtyła's personalistic ethic are briefly sketched in the opening pages of this book. It is difficult to argue with those premises. They are fully consistent with a long philosophical tradition that assumes man's rational nature by virtue of his spiritual soul. Thanks to the rational soul, every person has a natural dignity and enjoys superiority over other creatures, because only a person can think and will. This dignity is not some sort of social status to be bestowed but a universal reality that applies to every member of the human species. Unlike angelic or divine persons, the human person is also embodied, so he is a unique synthesis of matter and spirit. The alternative views are dualism (making two substances out of one) or materialism. Both theories deny the unity of the person, the "I" who thinks, acts, feels, and chooses as a body animated by a soul.[10]

---

9. Clarke, S.J., *Person and Being*, 76–80. Jacques Maritain was one of the first contemporary Thomists to speak in terms of this basic generosity of existence. See Jacques Maritain, *Existence and Existent* (New York: Doubleday, 1957), 90.

10. John Finnis, "On the Practical Meaning of Secularism," *Notre Dame Law Review* 73 (1998), 491.

The philosophy of materialism, which rejects the idea of a rational soul, cannot account for man's higher, spiritual activities such as his conceptual thought. A purely material being cannot grasp or understand universal, immaterial ideas, like a circle, that capture the meaning common to many instances of circles, nor can it understand abstract ideas like love and moral duty. If the products of human thought are spiritual, then the intellectual power which knows them must also be spiritual, and we call that spiritual entity a soul.[11]

Wojtyła's anthropology also overcomes the liabilities of dualism because it does justice to our embodiment in two ways in particular: 1) its emphasis on the body as a manifestation of the spirit, and 2) its insistence on man's natural wholeness as a body-soul unity. Wojtyła repeatedly explains that "the human body . . . constitutes a substantial unity with the human spirit" (p. 38). Competing theories that fall into the trap of dualism face the impossible task of explaining how and why the intellect cooperates with the body in the process of acquiring knowledge. The intellect works closely with the senses to help us grasp the structure or ordered patterns that are abstracted from material objects. This enables us to understand universal ideas, which express what is common to many particulars. After seeing several different dogs, for example, the mind grasps the universal idea of dog that applies to all of them despite their particular variations in size, shape, or breed. Moreover, if you are stabbed by someone wielding a knife, you don't say "my body was stabbed" but "I was stabbed." The person *is* his or her body. Anyone who harms the body harms the whole person. Thus, because we are embodied beings, a personal union must include a bodily union or it will not be comprehensive.[12] Similarly, since the body is an "integral part" of the person, it cannot be "separated from the totality of the person" to become an object for pleasure without an objectification of that whole person (p. 90).

Finally, if a person does have the capacities of reason and will thanks to the soul, it makes sense to describe personhood in terms of

---

11. Feser, *The Last Superstition*, 122–126.
12. Girgis, George, and Anderson, *What Is Marriage?*, 24.

self-possession. Because of his rationality, "man comprehends that he possesses himself" and is the master of his own actions (p. 207). We know from our own experience that because persons have self-awareness and self-determination, they are superior to all other creatures, which lack these capabilities. It follows, therefore, that the person should not be treated as an *object* of use but as a human *subject* who can think and choose for himself. Theories of sexual morality that are at odds with Catholic teaching or a personalist ethic quickly get derailed, because they disregard the fundamental structure of human nature in its non-dualistic integrity.

## Respect for persons

As we have seen, Wojtyła claims that following the personalistic norm is the best way to ensure that persons will be treated with the equal concern and respect they deserve. This norm affirms the unconditional value of the person, which is required by virtue of his special status as a spiritual being with an inner life. Unlike non-personal beings, each person has a natural dignity and intrinsic worth that does not depend on someone else's objectives. We must never treat persons as if they were things, merely as instrumental means to an end. On the contrary, we must respect their self-chosen ends, provided those ends are reasonable and proper to their nature. This norm plainly implies that there are some acts that defile the person and cannot be justified for any reason.

The personalistic norm is credible as a primary moral principle for at least two reasons. First, people naturally resist being used and manipulated by others for their selfish ends. This is certainly true in the area of sexual relations between men and women. Sexual shame poignantly reveals the "supra-utilitarian character of the person," who struggles against becoming an object of use even in another's interior desires or fantasies (p. 162). Second, this norm strictly prevents us from doing violence to other persons in body or spirit. Avoiding harm to others is fundamental to any sound ethical system. The norm can be easily defended so long as we appreciate that the person is an embodied spirit, not just a rational nature as Kant had supposed. Denying the validity of this normative principle opens up the prospect for many degrading offenses against humanity, such as slavery, meager wages, torture, and sex-trafficking in the name of some greater good or overriding objective. Using people in more moderate ways, even with their consent, still harms them because it undermines their sense of self-worth or self-respect. The virtue of self-respect is indispensable, since it disposes every person to the cultivation of other virtues and the pursuit of basic human goods that are aspects of human fulfillment.

The opposing theory of utilitarianism is a pragmatic system that has proven to be thoroughly inadequate in protecting each person's dignity because it tolerates the abuse of the person as a means to achieve a further end. Wojtyła's personalistic norm, however, provides a strong intellectual foundation for a sexual ethic based securely on the value and intrinsic worth of the human person.

Wojtyła harshly critiques hedonistic utilitarianism and similar ethical viewpoints that consider pleasure as a good or end in itself. The pursuit of pleasure for its own sake "clashes with the proper structure of human acts" (p. 20). Those acts aim at an intelligible good (such as health or friendship), and sometimes the achievement of what is truly good requires forgoing pleasure. Therefore, pleasure, unlike friendship or health, cannot be a good or end in itself. If pleasure were such an intelligible good, it would be possible to have a charitable disposition by willing pleasure for another (as his or her "true good"). If he or she does the same, the end result would be a form of fulfillment through mutual sexual satisfaction. But pleasure or emotional experience is only a side effect of our seeking out and realizing real basic goods that contribute to our human flourishing, such as health, knowledge, and friendship. Wojtyła describes pleasure as "something collateral, accidental, something that may occur when acting" (p. 20). Pleasure itself cannot fulfill us or perfect our human nature. We might think about it like this: what really matters to us is not the emotional satisfaction or pleasure that comes with friendship, but being a friend.[13] Being a

---

13. John Finnis, *Fundamentals of Ethics* (Washington, D.C.: Georgetown University Press, 1991), 47.

friend or coming to know the truth are always goods, because they promote our human flourishing. But some pleasures, like overeating or using heroin, are disordered because they harm us and undermine real goods like health. Moreover, as Wojtyła has pointed out, pleasure such as sexual satisfaction cannot be isolated from an act and considered to be a good. No one could say that although a sadist's activity is bad, the pleasure he derives from inflicting pain is good. Taking pleasure in harming other people is simply wrong. This sort of pleasure is woefully disordered.[14] Thus, because some pleasures are harmful, because pleasure is a mental state that happens to us as a byproduct of certain activities, pleasure cannot qualify as a basic or true human good.

Another key aspect of Wojtyła's argument is the assumption that sexuality has a natural purpose. We detect that purpose by looking at a human person's sexual design, including sexual complementarity. Here again it seems hard to quarrel with Wojtyła's insistence that the sexual drive itself and the sexual properties of a human being, which define that being as male or female, belong to our human nature. They are attributes of every person. We know from the animal world that the sexual drive has its own natural purpose, which means that it is directed to the end of reproduction. And that drive functions in human beings for the same purpose, that is, procreation. People do not construct the purpose of this drive, but find it in the fundamental structure of their human nature. At the same time, "the drive is subordinated to the person, and the person can use it at his discretion" (p. 33). This drive also represents a natural tendency to evolve into love, since it draws two persons into an intimate union. Hence, in the human person the purpose of our sexual capacities activated by this drive is both procreation *and* the union of a man and woman as a unique expression of spousal love.

Given these basic presuppositions and principles—the person as embodied spirit, the personalistic norm, the nature of love, the fact

---

14. Patrick Lee and Robert George, *Body-Self Dualism in Contemporary Ethics and Politics* (Cambridge: Cambridge University Press, 2008), 115.

that pleasure is not a basic human good, and the reality that sexual relations are inherently linked to procreation—it is easy to see how the rest of Wojtyła's argument hangs together. If we can't use a person for any reason, we must love and affirm that person for his or her own sake and care about that person's well-being. As a result, there is no way to justify sex with another purely for pleasure or enjoyment. Sex with someone simply for one's own pleasure is sensual egoism, not love. Even sex engaged in exclusively for mutual pleasure contradicts love, because love necessarily involves self-transcendence, a going beyond the self to affirm the beloved and to will his or her good. There is no authentic benevolence or mutual sharing, but only a self-centered focus on "getting" pleasure from this other person; any concern for the other's pleasure is conditioned on one's own self-gratification. In addition, since this type of sexual intercourse is almost always contraceptive, the couple's sexual powers are being used in a way that is inconsistent with their procreative purpose. Unless the sexual act is of the procreative type, expressing a full interpersonal union of a married couple, it necessarily involves selfish using for pleasure in violation of the personalistic norm.

In "deliberate 'free love,'" self-gratification and egoism substitute themselves for true love (p. 206). A promiscuous man, for example, typically sees in his partner an attractive body abstracted from a woman's personhood. His lust reduces the "whole personal richness of femininity" to her sexual attributes.[15] This type of "bodily love," which grows out of concupiscence, obscures the personhood of this woman and radically depersonalizes the sexual act. In such a sexual union, the body and its sexual values replace "the object of love, which is the person" (p. 132). As a result, both individuals are deprived of the great dignity of giving, expressed by their masculine and feminine bodies, which creates a fulfilling interpersonal communion. A sexual union, therefore, can only be justified as an expansion and expression of the "durable union of persons" that results from committed spousal love (p. 210).

---

15. John Paul II, *Man and Woman*, 288.

## Other moral issues

What are the other moral implications of Wojtyła's analysis? We have already considered the problem of positive contraception, but what about masturbation, cohabitation, and homosexual relations? We can readily discern the moral problem with these kinds of behavior in light of the personalistic norm and the objective order of nature. Solitary sex for the sake of pleasure is a misuse of one's bodily sexual powers. These powers exist for the purpose of procreation, and they are meant to serve as the way a person fully gives himself or herself to another in spousal love. In solitary sex, the body is instrumentalized for the sake of pleasure. The person treats himself as an object in violation of the personalistic norm. He sees himself not through the lens of personhood but "through the values of *sexus* alone as an 'object of possible use'" (p. 142). Masturbation is a capitulation to sensual egoism, a failure to respect the value of the person within one's own self. Hence, it cannot be as innocuous as some have carelessly suggested. Can a person who habitually seeks sexual satisfaction in this manner, thereby "wasting" love's "natural material," cultivate the capacity for marital intimacy (p. 133)? Can such a person come to see the body not as an object of use, but as a means of giving oneself to another?

Cohabitation makes extramarital sex habitual. It sometimes simulates a marital union but lacks the required commitment, since neither partner makes a total and exclusive mutual self-donation. Giving oneself only sexually without the full gift of one's person to validate that act leads only to selfish using of each other. There is a sexual union without a full interpersonal union. The couple's bodies are "striving" for an intimate "uniting of persons" (along with reproduction), but in their hearts they resist these goods (p. 78). Sexual union is meant to signify and embody a total sharing and exclusive commitment between two persons. But in this case it is a sham, because the sexual act does not express committed conjugal love directed at the true good of the beloved. Individuals who cohabitate are primarily seeking sexual pleasure as they weigh their options. So these relationships are characterized by mutual sexual exploitation rather than love, even though a couple may not realize that this is happening. Cohabitating couples sometimes think that the body and sexual intimacy by itself "possesses the key to the mystery of happiness" (p. 157). They must discover, however, that happiness can only be found in chaste spousal love that leads to marriage and family.

Finally, same-sex unions are morally problematic for many reasons, but most especially because they are not naturally procreative. These relations are in conflict with the "natural finality" of the sexual drive (p. 37). The purpose of our sexual powers is procreation; therefore they can only be used in a way that conforms to that purpose. As we have seen, sexual union must be an expression of "a union of persons in relation to *procreatio*" (p. 211). In order to complement their spiritual union of hearts and minds, a man and a woman form a bodily union, a complete whole that has reproduction as its end. But two same-sex partners cannot form such a union, since they cannot become biologically one in order to conceive a child. Despite the experience of intimacy, no total bodily communion of persons actually occurs. Without this unitive meaning associated with sexual difference and heterosexual intercourse, and without the common good of bearing and raising their own children in a familial community, the sexual relationship cannot meet the demands of the personalistic norm or the natural law. Man can only be faithful to the person "insofar as he is faithful to nature," and this fidelity requires respect for the "interior dynamic" of conjugal love with its openness to the "new good" of human life (p. 216). It can never be good for any person to use his or her sexual capacities in a way that is contrary to their purpose, which has been ordained by the Creator as part of the natural order. Two women or two men can show affection for each other and fortify their commitment as friends in many non-sexual ways. Any sexual activity that is non-unitive and non-procreative can only have pleasure or sexual satisfaction as a motive.[16]

It is important to point out, however, the Catholic Church's distinction between the homosexual condition and homosexual acts. Only the latter are considered sinful. Moreover, the Church does not single out

---

16. See Grisez, *Living a Christian Life*, 653. I am indebted to Grisez's discussion on sexual morality, which I have relied upon throughout the latter part of this concluding chapter.

the sexual sin of sodomy but groups it together with the unchaste acts of heterosexual couples that are acts against the good of marriage. All sexual activities outside of marriage, "'adultery' in the broadest sense," are considered morally evil, in violation of the Decalogue and the Gospel (p. 205). As we have explained, even sexual activity within marriage must be justified in God's eyes. Wojtyła repeatedly underscores that "conjugal intercourse must be permeated with a readiness for parenthood" (p. 235). Thus, in keeping with the teaching of *Love and Responsibility*, homosexual men and women are called to live chastely and should be able to count on their fellow Christians for compassion and support.[17]

These high ethical standards that confine sexual activity to marriage have become increasingly countercultural in our secular environment. Many people have abandoned such a strict sexual morality despite its rational coherence. Even some moral theologians assert that our ability to remain chaste or to sustain a permanent marital commitment is heavily compromised in today's hypersexualized culture. But the Catholic Church itself continues to hold firm to its convictions. It is not afraid to be countercultural because Jesus himself was a "sign of contradiction," as we are told in Luke's Gospel (2:35). In one of his encyclicals, John Paul II explained that while Catholic moral teaching is challenging, it is certainly not "unattainable." The fatalistic attitude that chastity or a lifelong, fruitful marriage is beyond our reach overlooks the powers of grace and redemption. Thanks to our adoption as sons and daughters of God, we have at our disposal an abundance of divine graces to help us live up to our high moral calling. The fact that we have been redeemed by Christ makes all the difference, because it means that our weak human nature has been healed and sanctified by grace. God's commands in the area of sexuality are difficult but not impossible. As John Paul II tells us, we must realize that this command is "proportioned to man's capabilities, but to the capabilities of man to whom the Holy

---

17. Germain Grisez, *Difficult Moral Questions* (Quincy, IL: Franciscan Press, 1997), 103–110. See also John Harvey, O.S.F.S., *The Truth about Homosexuality: The Cry of the Faithful* (San Francisco: Ignatius Press, 1996).

Spirit has been given."[18] Hence, through prayer, fasting, and frequent reception of the sacraments, we must seek out the Holy Spirit's help so that we can live chastely and give generously.

## Conclusion

It would be instructive to elaborate further on how this convincing theory of sexual morality put forth in *Love and Responsibility* bears on other specific issues that currently dominate the moral landscape. Although more could be said about these matters, this study will conclude here because its main task is complete. It has explained and evaluated the general sense of Wojtyła's "integral vision," which demonstrates the synthesis of romantic or erotic love and the virtue of charity (p. xxiii). Authentic spousal love, which precludes sexual union outside of marriage, does justice to both the creative energy of the sexual drive and the Gospel commandment to love that is the "main bond of the whole supernatural order" (p. xxiii). Wojtyła has presented an original and highly plausible approach to sexual ethics, revolving around the personalistic norm and the natural moral order, which touches deep nerves of truth. Some of the ideas here are quite familiar, and all of them are consistent with Catholic teachings. However, Wojtyła has taken a new road, exploring the nuances of sexual morality through the lens of personalism, set within the frame of a metaphysical perspective. Along the way, he has opened new horizons for reflecting on the interrelated themes of personhood, love, chastity, and marriage. We are constantly reminded here about the "natural greatness" and grandeur of marriage, which remains one of the greatest possibilities that life has to offer us (p. 110).

To be sure, the intellectual forces of pragmatism and relativism that seek to undermine traditional marriage have not lost their momentum. Any effort to reverse course will encounter powerful resistance. The

---

18. John Paul II, *Veritatis Splendor*, §103.

intellectual fissures that separate secular culture from the authentic "culture of the person" continue to deepen (p. 218). For any hope of success in this ambient environment, there must be a radical intellectual conversion. Faith will need the close cooperation of reason to revive a sexual morality firmly anchored in the vision of spousal love articulated in this book. Karol Wojtyła, who became the Pope from a "far country" in 1978, performed a great service in writing this treatise. It certainly seems impolitic in light of today's permissive standards. However, this bold work is a wise and balanced reflection that confirms the words of Jesus himself, along with the whole biblical witness to morally acceptable sexual mores.

# Further Reading

## Works by Karol Wojtyła

*Love and Responsibility.* Translated by Grzegorz Ignatik. Boston: Pauline Books & Media, 2013.

*Person and Community: Selected Essays.* Translated by T. Sandok. New York: Peter Lang, 1993.

*The Jeweler's Shop.* Translated by Boleslaw Taborski. San Francisco: Ignatius Press, 1992.

*Faith According to St. John of the Cross.* San Francisco: St. Ignatius Press, 1981.

*Sources of Renewal: The Implementation of the Vatican Council.* New York: Collins, 1980.

*Sign of Contradiction.* New York: Seabury Press, 1979.

*The Acting Person.* Translated by A. Potocki. Dordrecht: D. Reidel Publishing, 1979.

# Works by John Paul II

*Man and Woman He Created Them: A Theology of the Body*. Translated by Michael Waldstein. Boston: Pauline Books & Media, 2006.

*Memory and Identity*. New York: Rizzoli International Publishers, 2005.

*Rise, Let Us Be On Our Way*. New York: Warner Books, 2004.

*The Splendor of Truth: Encyclical Letter (Veritatis Splendor)*. Boston: Pauline Books & Media, 2003.

*Gift and Mystery*. New York: Doubleday, 1997.

*Crossing the Threshold of Hope*. New York: Alfred A. Knopf, 1994.

*Letter to Families*. Boston: Pauline Books & Media, 1994.

*On the Family: Apostolic Exhortation (Familiaris Consortio)*. Boston: Pauline Books & Media, 1981.

# Works on *Love and Responsibility*

Crosby, John. "Karol Wojtyła's Personalist Understanding of Man and Woman." In *Personalist Papers*. Ed. John Crosby. Washington, D.C.: Catholic University of America Press, 2004: 243–263.

De Lestapis, Joseph. "A Summary of Karol Wojtyła's *Love and Responsibility*." In *Christian Married Living*. Ed. R. Dennehy. San Francisco: Ignatius Press, 1981: 101–132.

Farauanu, Leonard. "The Immorality of Contraception According to *Love and Responsibility* of Karol Wojtyła," Studia Theologica 5.1 (2007): 42–50.

Grondelski, John. "The Fiftieth Anniversary of *Love and Responsibility*: An Appreciation." *FCS Quarterly* Winter (2010): 25–29.

May, William. "Karol Wojtyła's *Love and Responsibility:* A Summary." Available at: http://www.christendom-awake.org/pages/may/summaryofl&r.htm.

O'Leary, Joseph. "John Paul II on *Love and Responsibility*." *Furrow* 29 (1979): 735–741.

Page, Jean-Guy. "La Pensée de Karol Wojtyła sur la Relation Homme-Femme." *Laval Théologique et Philosophique* 40.1 (1984): 3–29.

Smith, Janet. "Responsible Parenthood as Conscious Parenthood." *Familia et Vita* 14 (2009): 144–156.

Spinello, Richard. "The Rehabilitation of Chastity." *Homiletic and Pastoral Review.* February (2011): 58–64.

Sri, Edward. *Men, Women, and the Mystery of Love: Practical Insights from John Paul II's* Love and Responsibility. Cincinnati: Servant Books, 2007.

Walsh, Vincent. *Love and Responsibility: A Simplified Version.* Philadelphia: Key of David Publishers, 2001.

## General Works

Allegri, Renzo. *John Paul II: A Life of Grace.* Cincinnati: Servant Books, 2005.

Aquinas, St. Thomas. *Summa Theologiae.* 5 volumes (New York: Benziger Bros., 1948).

Boniecki, Adam, ed. *Kalendarium of the Life of Karol Wojtyła.* Stockbridge, MA: Marian Press, 2000.

Budziszewski, J. *On the Meaning of Sex.* Wilmington: ISI Books, 2012.

Buttiglione, Rocco. *Karol Wojtyła: The Thought of the Man Who Became Pope John Paul II.* Grand Rapids, MI: Eerdmans Publishing, 1997.

*Catechism of the Catholic Church.* New York: Doubleday, 1995.

Clarke, W. Norris, S.J. *Explorations in Metaphysics.* Notre Dame: University of Notre Dame Press, 1994.

———. *Person and Being.* Milwaukee: Marquette University Press, 1993.

Feser, Edward. *The Last Superstition.* South Bend, IN: St. Augustine's Press, 2010.

Finnis, John. *Fundamentals of Ethics*. Washington, D.C.: Georgetown University Press, 1991.

Franks, Angela. *Contraception and Catholicism*. Boston: Pauline Books & Media, 2013.

Fromm, Erich. *The Art of Loving*. New York: Harper, 2006. (Original edition, 1956).

Girgis, Sherif, Ryan Anderson, and Robert George. *What Is Marriage? Man and Woman: A Defense*. New York: Encounter Books, 2012.

Gneuhs, G., ed. *The Legacy of Pope John Paul II*. New York: Crossroad, 2000.

Grisez, Germain. *Living a Christian Life*. Quincy, IL: Franciscan Press, 1993.

Hogan, Richard and John LeVoir. *Covenant of Love*. San Francisco: Ignatius Press, 1992.

Kant, Immanuel. *Foundations of the Metaphysics of Morals*. Translated by Lewis Beck. Indianapolis: Bobbs-Merrill, 1959.

Lee, Patrick and Robert George. *Body-Self Dualism in Contemporary Ethics and Politics*. Cambridge: Cambridge University Press, 2008.

Lee, Patrick. "Marriage, Procreation and Same-Sex Unions." *The Monist*. 91(3) (2008): 427–35.

Lewis, C. S. *The Four Loves*. New York: Houghton-Mifflin, 1988.

May, Rollo. *Love and Will*. New York: Dell Publishing, 1969.

May, William. *Theology of the Body in Context: Genesis and Growth*. Boston: Pauline Books and Media, 2010.

Pruss, Alexander. *One Body: An Essay in Christian Sexual Ethics*. Notre Dame: University of Notre Dame Press, 2013.

Scola, Angelo. *The Nuptial Mystery*. Translated by M. Borras. Grand Rapids, MI: Eerdmans, 2005.

Shivanandan, Mary. *Crossing the Threshold of Love*. Washington, D.C.: Catholic University of America Press, 1999.

Simpson, Peter. *Karol Wojtyła*. New York: Wadsworth, 2002.

Smith, Janet, ed. *Why Humanae Vitae Was Right: A Reader*. San Francisco: Ignatius Press, 1993.

Spinello, Richard. *The Encyclicals of John Paul II: An Introduction and Commentary*. Lanham, MD: Rowman & Littlefield, 2012.

————. *The Genius of John Paul II: The Great Pope's Moral Wisdom*. Lanham, MD: Sheed & Ward, 2007.

Von Hildebrand, Dietrich. *The Nature of Love*. Translated by John Crosby. South Bend, IN: St. Augustine's Press, 2009.

Weigel, George. *The End and the Beginning*. New York: Doubleday, 2010.

————. *Witness to Hope*. New York: Harper Collins, 1999.

Williams, George H. *The Mind of John Paul II*. New York: Seabury, 1981.

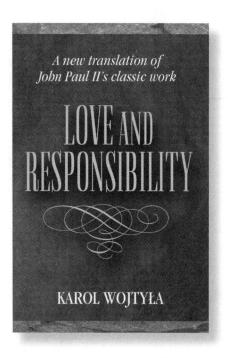

## Love and Responsibility

A new translation of John Paul II's classic work

Karol Wojtyła

Originally published in Polish in 1960, *Love and Responsibility* is Karol Wojtyła's groundbreaking book on human love. In this classic work, Wojtyła explains relationships between persons, especially concerning sexual ethics, in the perspective of the true meaning of love. Grzegorz Ignatik, a native Polish speaker, has translated the 2001 version of the text, which includes revisions made by Blessed John Paul II himself of the original 1960 edition, providing helpful notes and defining key terms.

Paperback, 384 pages
0-8198-4558-2      9780819845580
$24.95 USD

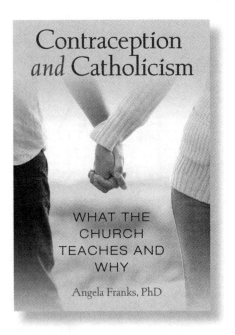

## Contraception and Catholicism
### What the Church Teaches and Why
#### Angela Franks, PhD

Providing a comprehensive understanding of the Catholic Church's teaching on contraception, Angela Franks, PhD, an experienced pro-life speaker and educator, explores how to live in accordance with Catholic sexual teaching and equips readers with the knowledge to explain the teaching to others. This understanding addresses Church history and the prevailing ideologies of today's mainstream society. Sociological data, vignettes of real life couples, a brief summary of natural family planning (NFP) and NaPRO Technology, and allusions to Theology of the Body are included.

Paperback, 136 pages
0-8198-1638-8     9780819816382
$7.95 USD

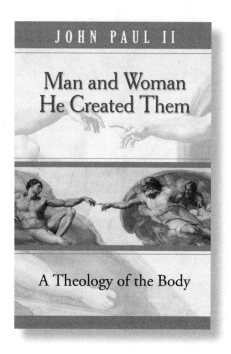

## Man and Woman He Created Them
### A Theology of the Body
#### Written by John Paul II

Translation, introduction,
and index by Michael Waldstein

Internationally renowned Biblical scholar Michael Waldstein offers a new critical translation of Pope John Paul II's talks on the Theology of the Body, presenting his magnificent vision of the human person with meticulous scholarship and profound insight. A preface by Cardinal Schönborn, a foreword by Christopher West, a comprehensive index of words and phrases, a Scriptural index, and a reference table for other versions of the papal texts are included. Recipient of a CPA Award!

Paperback, 768 pages
0-8198-7421-3     9780819874214
$29.95 USD

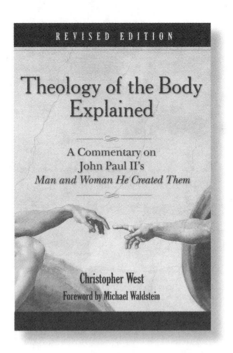

## Theology of the Body Explained

A Commentary on John Paul II's
*Man and Woman He Created Them*

Christopher West

In this revised and expanded edition of his best-selling *Theology of the Body Explained* (2003), Christopher West illuminates John Paul II's Theology of the Body. This revised edition incorporates all of the changes discovered by Michael Waldstein's outstanding translation of John Paul II's catechesis: *Man and Woman He Created Them: A Theology of the Body*, including the newly discovered addresses on the Song of Songs, Tobit, and Ephesians—unfolded here for the first time.

Paperback, 688 pages
0-8198-7425-6     9780819874252
$29.95 USD

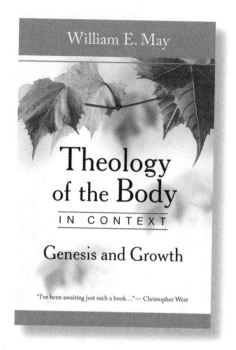

## Theology of the Body in Context
### Genesis and Growth
### William E. May

The zenith of John Paul II's thought on the human person, marriage, and the family is found in his Theology of the Body. For the first time, William E. May provides a comprehensive yet readable overview of this work in the context of several other key writings of Karol Wojtyła/John Paul II—including *Love and Responsibility*, *Familiaris Consortio*, *Mulieris Dignitatem*, and *Letter to Families*—providing rich insights into the development of his Theology of the Body.

Paperback, 176 pages
0-8198-7431-0     9780819874313
$16.95 USD

## The Theology of the Body Made Simple
### Anthony Percy

This is a simple introduction to John Paul II's basic premise of the Theology of the Body. It explains how our bodies are symbolic, free, meant for love, and redeemed by Christ. It presents unambiguous reasons for the Church's teaching on premarital sex, contraception, homosexuality, pornography, and more. And it gives reason to hope that the love we crave so deeply is, in fact, promised us by God—from the beginning.

Paperback, 112 pages
0-8198-7419-1     9780819874191
$9.95 USD

## The Human Person

According to John Paul II

J. Brian Bransfield

In the 20th century, three social revolutions—industrial, sexual, and techno-logical—challenged the religious convictions of many. John Paul II's teaching on the Theology of the Body was his response to the resulting societal shifts. J. Brian Bransfield explores John Paul II's reactions to the challenges raised by these revolutions. Within this context, Bransfield then explores how Theology of the Body insights lead us to live the fullness of the Christian life.

Paperback, 288 pages
0-8198-3394-0    9780819833945
$19.95 USD

**BOOKS & MEDIA**

A mission of the Daughters of St. Paul

As apostles of Jesus Christ, evangelizing today's world:

We are CALLED to holiness
by God's living Word and Eucharist.

We COMMUNICATE the Gospel message
through our lives and through all
available forms of media.

We SERVE the Church
by responding to the hopes and needs
of all people with the Word of God,
in the spirit of St. Paul.

For more information visit our website: www.pauline.org.

**BOOKS & MEDIA**

The Daughters of St. Paul operate book and media centers at the following addresses. Visit, call, or write the one nearest you today, or find us at www.pauline.org.

## CALIFORNIA

| | |
|---|---|
| 3908 Sepulveda Blvd, Culver City, CA 90230 | 310-397-8676 |
| 935 Brewster Avenue, Redwood City, CA 94063 | 650-369-4230 |
| 5945 Balboa Avenue, San Diego, CA 92111 | 858-565-9181 |

## FLORIDA
145 S.W. 107th Avenue, Miami, FL 33174     305-559-6715

## HAWAII
1143 Bishop Street, Honolulu, HI 96813     808-521-2731

## ILLINOIS
172 North Michigan Avenue, Chicago, IL 60601     312-346-4228

## LOUISIANA
4403 Veterans Memorial Blvd, Metairie, LA 70006     504-887-7631

## MASSACHUSETTS
885 Providence Hwy, Dedham, MA 02026     781-326-5385

## MISSOURI
9804 Watson Road, St. Louis, MO 63126     314-965-3512

## NEW YORK
64 W. 38th Street, New York, NY 10018     212-754-1110

## SOUTH CAROLINA
243 King Street, Charleston, SC 29401     843-577-0175

## VIRGINIA
1025 King Street, Alexandria, VA 22314     703-549-3806

## CANADA
3022 Dufferin Street, Toronto, ON M6B 3T5     416-781-9131

¡También somos su fuente para libros,
videos y música en español!